LIVEWIRE
REAL LIVES

Learner Services

Please return
on or before
the last date
stamped below

CITY COLLEGE
NORWICH

- 3 JUN 2009

0 5 MAR 2012

2 7 NOV 2012

Pu   :y

A MEMBER OF THE HODDER HEADLINE GROUP

The Publishers would like to thank the following for permission to reproduce copyright material:

Photo credits
pp.3, 21 © Action Images; pp.10, 14, 17, 24 © Colorsport; p.27 © Matthew Ashton/ Empics.

The text of this book is not in any way endorsed by Arsenal Football Club.

Orders: please contact Bookpoint Ltd, 130 Milton Park, Abingdon, Oxon OX14 4SB. Telephone (44) 01235 827720. Fax: (44) 01235 400454. Lines are open from 9.00–5.00, Monday to Saturday, with a 24-hour message answering service. You can also order through our website www.hoddereducation.co.uk

Cover photo © Carl de Souza/AFP/Getty Images
Typeset in 14pt Palatino by SX Composing DTP, Rayleigh, Essex.
Printed in Great Britain by CPI Bath.

A catalogue record for this title is available from the British Library

ISBN-10 0 340 90074 1
ISBN-13 978 0 340 90074 1

Contents

1 'They used to be great!'

'Arsenal used to be a great team.'
That's what people say about Arsenal.
They say,
'Once Arsenal was the best team
in the country.'
Then they sigh,
and shake their heads.
'But it's not true now,'
they say.

They've always said that about Arsenal.
If Arsenal win the Cup, they say,
'It must be luck,
because they're not as good as they used to be!'
If Arsenal win the League, they say,
'They used to be better!'
And if Arsenal win the Double, they say,
'Not bad!
But the old team was really great!'

1

So Arsenal know
that whatever they do,
they'll never, ever,
be as good as they used to be!

But the people do have a point,
because back in the 'good old days' of football,
Arsenal was the best team in the country,
for year after year after year.

The 'good old days' of football,
when players wore grandad vests
and long flannel shorts.
When shinpads were as thick as planks,
and boots as stiff as boards.
When the ball was heavy, brown leather,
and the ground was a muddy field.
When the players were miners or bricklayers
during the week,
and only played on Saturday.
They earned four pounds a week,
and thought themselves lucky!
The good old days of football,
that's when Arsenal were great!

The 'good old days' of football.
Arsenal v Liverpool.
FA Cup Final, 1950.

You can still see them in the old photographs,
hard men with moustaches and bony knees,
and managers with straw hats and watch-chains.
That's when Arsenal were great!

They were formed in 1886.
They are one of the oldest clubs in the country.
They were formed by men
who worked in the arsenal
in Woolwich in London.

An arsenal is where guns are made,
and the team has been called the Gunners
ever since.
Their proper name was the Royal Arsenal,
then the Woolwich Arsenal,
and then just Arsenal.

In 1913, they moved to Highbury,
which is still their ground.
Also in 1913,
they were relegated!

There's nothing wrong with that.
All clubs get relegated sometimes,
and come back up again.
But with Arsenal this is the only time
it has ever happened!

They have been in the Premier Division
longer than anyone else.

2 Herbert Chapman

The glory years started for Arsenal in 1925.
Herbert Chapman became manager.
He changed the club completely.

In nine years they won the League five times
and the Cup twice.
They weren't just
the most famous team in England,
they were also
the most famous team in the world!
In fact during this time
the Arsenal football team was more famous
than the England football team.

Years later, great players
from Europe and South America
said they used to read about Arsenal
and see their picture in the paper.

This was because Herbert Chapman
was so good at advertising.
He made sure the name 'Arsenal'
was always in the news.
He even got a London tube station
named after the team!

He was the first modern manager,
as famous as the team itself.

He also brought
lots of new things into the game
that we take for granted now –
numbers on players' shirts,
floodlighting, and white balls.

He was good
at getting the best from the players.
One said afterwards,
'Chapman knew when to blow you up
and when to blow you down,
when to be the Big Boss
and when to be the Family Friend.
He was a genius,
and that's the fact of it.'

He made the team play round a 'stopper'.
This was a defender
who didn't have any position.
But he supported the defence
wherever it was needed.
This made Arsenal very difficult to beat.
Even if Arsenal didn't score many goals,
nobody could score against them.
This way of playing can work,
but it is very dull!
People started saying
Arsenal is a dull team.
They still say that today!

Herbert Chapman died in 1935.
A statue was made of him,
and his special seat preserved.
They do say
that down the corridors of the old club,
when things are going badly for them,
you can still see his ghost
urging the team on.

The captain of Arsenal at this time
was Eddie Hapgood.
He was also captain of England.
While he was captain of England,
he was at the centre of a very famous story.

Eddie Hapgood, captain of Arsenal, before the war.

England were playing Germany.
It was before the war,
and Hitler was in charge of Germany.
The team was told
they had to give the Nazi salute.
Eddie Hapgood said the team wouldn't,
but they were told they had to.
The British Ambassador said,
'If I do it,
why shouldn't you or your team?'
So the team did.
They stood there with their arms raised
in the Nazi salute.
When the pictures were seen in the papers,
everyone was angry.

They blamed Eddie Hapgood.
He said,
'We gave them the best answer we could.
We won 6–3.'

Everybody knows this story.
People still argue about it.
But not so many know that the next day
Aston Villa also played in Germany.
They were told
they had to give the Nazi salute as well.
But they wouldn't.
They did give a salute,
but it was two fingers!

But then they lost!

3 Billy Wright

After the great days of Herbert Chapman,
it was a long time
before Arsenal won anything again.
They tried lots of managers,
but none of them settled.

One of them was Billy Wright.
He had been captain of England,
and the most popular player in England.
He was married to one of the Beverley Sisters.
They were famous singers at the time.

Billy Wright chaired off the field in victory.
England v Scotland, 1959.

The Beverley Sisters had a hit called,
'How Much is that Doggie in the Window?'
It went:

'How much is that doggie in the window?
woof, woof!
The one with the wagg-er-ly tail?
woof, woof!
How much is that doggie in the window?
woof, woof!
I do hope that doggie's for sale!'

At every match the fans used to sing this song.
But they changed the words!!

Billy Wright did lots of good things
for Arsenal.
He brought on a lot of young players.
But he didn't last long.

Soon after Billy Wright left,
people said again
that Arsenal were playing dull football.

4 Bertie Mee

It wasn't until 1966
that things started to look up for Arsenal.
They appointed Bertie Mee as manager.

He was a quiet man,
but he knew how to get the best
out of a player.

In 1970, Arsenal won the European Fairs Cup,
which was their first 'big' cup for 17 years.

But 1971 was the really big year for Arsenal.
They won the Double:
the League and the Cup.
It was the first time for them,
and only four other clubs have done it.

The rock star footballer.
Charlie George, 1971.

Bob Wilson was the goalkeeper.
He went to work in television
when he retired.

There was also George Graham,
but the real star was Charlie George.

Charlie George had long hair
right over his shoulders.
He looked more like a rock star
than a footballer.
It was the first time
a footballer had hair like that.

Everybody knew Charlie George!

They knew him even better
after the Cup Final!
It was against Liverpool.
It was a really dull game.
Neither side would give anything.
It went to extra time.
Liverpool scored straight away,
and everyone thought,
'That's it! Liverpool have won!'

But then Arsenal scored.
It was 1–1!
Would it be a replay?

And then in the last seconds,
the ball was passed to Charlie George.
He was a long way outside the penalty area.
There didn't seem to be any danger.
But he shot,
and scored.
A goal that is still shown on television
as a goal of the century.

In 1979, Arsenal won the Cup again,
in one of the most exciting finishes ever
in a Cup Final.

They were playing Manchester United.
Arsenal were winning 2–0
until just four minutes from the end.
Then United scored,
not once, but twice,
seconds before the end.

It would be extra time!

Liam Brady wearing his winning hat.
Arsenal v Manchester United.
FA Cup Final, 1979.

Arsenal looked tired.
They had been winning
all through the game,
and they were shocked by the goals.

United looked excited and eager.
They were certain they could win
in extra time.
But Arsenal refused to be beaten.
Liam Brady passed to Graham Rix
from the kick-off.
Rix sent over a perfect cross
for Alan Sunderland to score.
Pat Rice, the Arsenal captain,
lifted the 1979 FA Cup.

5 George Graham

George Graham had been a player
in the Double team of 1971.
In 1986, he was made manager.

Soon the results started to get better.
They won the League Cup in 1987,
and the League itself in 1989 and 1991.
In 1993, they won the League Cup and the FA Cup.
A different sort of double.
And in 1994, Arsenal took home
the European Cup Winners' Cup.

Everything looked good for Arsenal.
The goalkeeper was David Seaman,
the best in the country.
The strikers were Paul Merson and Ian Wright,
who had been top goal scorers in the League.
All of them played for England.
And George Graham
had been Manager of the Year twice.

Ian Wright celebrates with George Graham, the manager.
Arsenal v Sheffield Wednesday.
FA Cup Final, 1993.

But then it all went wrong!

It was something to do with
money and transfers.
Nobody really knows the truth.
George Graham was accused
of 'improper conduct'.
He said he was innocent,
but he couldn't prove it.
The club had to sack him,
and he was banned for a year.

And then Paul Merson was caught taking drugs.
He was one of the great stars of Arsenal,
even though he was also an alcoholic,
and hooked on gambling.

But he has tried hard
to overcome his problems
and play good football.
He is now a player/manager
for Walsall Football Club.

But all these problems
had upset the team.

They didn't settle until 1996,
when Arsène Wenger became coach.
By 1999 he had built a new team
around Thierry Henry, the French striker.

By 2000, they had become
the top team in England.
And they have stayed the top team in England.
They were unbeaten for 49 matches.
No other club has done that in modern times.

They have won every trophy
except the big one –
the UEFA Champions' League.

If they do win it,
then at last Arsenal will be
as good as they used to be.

The Arsenal team after winning the FA Cup Final in 2002.

Human Kinetics

247 588

Library of Congress Cataloging-in-Publication Data

Kirkendall, Donald T.
  Soccer anatomy / Donald T. Kirkendall.
    p. cm.
  ISBN-13: 978-0-7360-9569-3 (soft cover)
  ISBN-10: 0-7360-9569-1 (soft cover)
  1. Soccer--Training. 2. Soccer--Physiological aspects. I. Title.
  GV943.9.T7K57 2011
  796.334--dc22

                          2011011402

ISBN-10: 0-7360-9569-1 (print)
ISBN-13: 978-0-7360-9569-3 (print)

This publication is written and published to provide accurate and authoritative information relevant to the subject matter presented. It is published and sold with the understanding that the author and publisher are not engaged in rendering legal, medical, or other professional services by reason of their authorship or publication of this work. If medical or other expert assistance is required, the services of a competent professional person should be sought.

The web addresses cited in this text were current as of May 2011 unless otherwise noted.

Acquisitions Editor: Tom Heine; **Developmental Editor:** Cynthia McEntire; **Assistant Editors:** Laura Podeschi, Claire Gilbert; **Copyeditor:** Patricia MacDonald; **Graphic Designer:** Fred Starbird; **Graphic Artist:** Tara Welsch; **Cover Designer:** Keith Blomberg; **Photographer (for soccer illustration references):** Tony Quinn; **Photographer (for exercise illustration references):** Peter Mueller; **Visual Production Assistant:** Joyce Brumfield; **Art Manager:** Kelly Hendren; **Illustration (cover):** Jen Gibas; **Illustrations (interior):** Precision Graphics; **Printer:** Premier Print Group

Human Kinetics books are available at special discounts for bulk purchase. Special editions or book excerpts can also be created to specification. For details, contact the Special Sales Manager at Human Kinetics.

Printed in the United States of America   10   9   8   7   6   5   4   3   2   1

Human Kinetics
website: www.HumanKinetics.com

United States: Human Kinetics
P.O. Box 5076
Champaign, IL 61825-5076
800-747-4457
e-mail: humank@hkusa.com

Canada: Human Kinetics
475 Devonshire Road Unit 100
Windsor, ON N8Y 2L5
800-465-7301 (in Canada only)
e-mail: info@hkcanada.com

Europe: Human Kinetics
107 Bradford Road
Stanningley
Leeds LS28 6AT, United Kingdom
+44 (0) 113 255 5665
e-mail: hk@hkeurope.com

Australia: Human Kinetics
57A Price Avenue
Lower Mitcham, South Australia 5062
08 8372 0999
e-mail: info@hkaustralia.com

New Zealand: Human Kinetics
P.O. Box 80
Torrens Park, South Australia 5062
0800 222 062
e-mail: info@hknewzealand.com

E5190

CONTENTS

PREFACE

Pele called it "the beautiful game." The simplicity of his comment about soccer has resonated among fans of the game for decades. The beauty of soccer begins with skill. Beautiful soccer means controlling an impossible ball, such as Dennis Bergkamp's 89th-minute goal in the 1998 FIFA World Cup or Maxi Rodriguez's chest-to-volley strike from the upper corner of the penalty area at the 2006 FIFA World Cup. Soccer's beauty is in the perfectly paced seeing-eye pass threaded through the smallest opening in the defense, which you will see anytime Kaka (Brazil) or Xavi (Spain) is playing. Or a solo dribbling run through the defense such as Diego Maradona's 1v7 run against England in the 1986 FIFA World Cup. Or the long-range cannon shot by Paul Breitner at the 1974 FIFA World Cup.

Then there is tactical brilliance. How about the 25-pass sequence to a goal by Argentina against Serbia in the 2006 FIFA World Cup, or the lightning-fast length-of-the-field counterattack for a goal by the United States against Brazil in the 2009 FIFA Confederations Cup final? Brazil's fourth goal against Italy in the 1970 World Cup is still considered a masterful display of teamwork, skill, and guile.

The objective of soccer is the same as in any other team sport: Score more than the opponent. This simple philosophy is enormously complicated. To be successful, a team must be able to present a physical, technical, tactical, and psychological display that is superior to the opponent's. When these elements work in concert, soccer is indeed a beautiful game. But when one aspect is not in sync with the rest, a team can be masterful and still lose. The British say, "They played well and died in beauty."

Soccer, like baseball, has suffered under some historical inertia: "We've never done that before and won. Why change?" or "I never did that stuff when I played." That attitude is doomed to limit the development of teams and players as the physical and tactical demands of the game advance.

And oh how the game has advanced. For example, the first reports on running distance during a match noted English professionals of the mid 1970s (Everton FC) averaged about 8,500 meters (5.5 miles). Today, most distances average between 10,000 and 14,000 meters (6 and 8.5 miles). There are reports that females, with their smaller hearts, lower hemoglobin levels, and smaller muscle mass, can cover the 6 miles attributed to men. The distance and number of runs at high speed have also increased as the pace of the game has become more ballistic and powerful. To those of us who have followed the game over the years, the pros sure do seem to strike the ball a lot harder now.

But the benefits of soccer extend beyond the competitive game. Emerging evidence shows that regular participation in soccer by adults is as effective as traditional aerobic exercise such as jogging for general health and for treating certain chronic conditions. For example, people with hypertension can see reductions in blood pressure similar to that seen in joggers. Blood fats can be reduced. Increased insulin sensitivity means those with type 2 diabetes and metabolic syndrome should see benefits. Regular soccer helps people, youths or adults, who are attempting to lose weight. A host of benefits are possible, all from playing an enjoyable game. An interesting sidenote is that when those studies were concluded, a lot of joggers just quit, but soccer players looked at each other and said, "Great. Can we go play now?"

The game is not as embedded in American culture as it is in other countries. Around the world, families, neighbors, and friends play the game whenever they can. In the United States, this neverending exposure to soccer is not as evident, so upon joining a team, an American child does not possess the beginnings of a skill set obtained from free play with family and friends. The coach may well be the child's only exposure to the game, requiring almost all coaching to be focused on the ball, which may neglect some basic motor skills and supplementary aspects of fitness.

In particular, the soccer community—and not just in the United States—has viewed supplemental strength training with skepticism. In addition, soccer players tend to view any running that is longer than the length of a field as unnecessary, and they avoid training that does not involve the ball. But give them a ball and they will run all day. The problem is many coaches apply the principle of specificity of training too literally ("if you want to be a better soccer player, play soccer") and end up denying players training benefits that are proven to improve physical performance and prevent injury.

This book is about supplemental strength training for soccer. When developed properly, increased strength will allow players to run faster, resist challenges, be stronger in the tackle, jump higher, avoid fatigue, and prevent injury. Most soccer players have a negative attitude toward strength training because it is done in a weight room and does not involve the ball. These attitudes were taken into consideration when the exercises in this book were selected. Many can be done on the field during routine training, and some involve the ball.

When a player or coach does favor some strength training, the primary focus is usually the legs. But as any strength and conditioning specialist will tell you, a balance must be struck up and down the body because the body is a link of segments, chains if you will, and the most prepared player will have addressed each link of the chain, not just an isolated link or two. Furthermore, those same specialists will say that while one group of muscles may be important within a sport, to address that group alone and neglect the opposite group of muscles will result in an imbalance around that movement or joint. Imbalances are known to raise the risk of injury. It has been known for years that strong quadriceps and weak hamstrings increase the risk of knee injury, but it is also known that athletes with a history of hamstring injury not only have weak hamstrings but also have poor function in the gluteal muscles. Weak hamstrings are also implicated in low back issues.

Many readers will review these exercises and select those that address specific weaknesses. The exercises in *Soccer Anatomy* are good choices to supplement traditional soccer training, but the concepts continue to evolve. These exercises are a good place to begin. With a regular program that uses systematic progression, players will improve aspects of fitness important for competitive play—aspects not addressed in traditional ball-oriented training. Players who want to keep playing and stay healthy with as few injuries as possible need to include some strength training. Players who neglect the strength element of training but want to move up to the next level will be in for a shock when they discover how far behind they are and realize just how much catching up is necessary. Should these exercises be considered the definitive list? Of course they shouldn't. Will conditioning professionals offer alternatives? Of course they will. But this is a good starting point with options for the coach and player.

The unique aspect of *Soccer Anatomy* isn't the supplemental exercises, as many other resources can provide suggestions. *Soccer Anatomy* takes you inside each exercise to show you which muscles are involved and how they contribute to proper execution of the exercise and to success on the field. The anatomical illustrations that accompany the exercises are color coded to indicate the primary and secondary muscles featured in each exercise and movement.

■ Primary muscles   ☐ Secondary muscles

Use this information to improve your skill, build your strength and endurance, and stay on the pitch. Choose exercises that are appropriate for your age, gender, experience, and training goals. Even young athletes can benefit from resistance training. In preadolescent athletes, strength improvements come mostly from increasing training volume by adding repetitions and sets while using modest resistance (e.g., two or three sets of 12 to 15 repetitions on two or three nonconsecutive days per week). Excellent exercise choices for preadolescents are those that use body weight for resistance.

Resistance training, like any physical training, has inherent risks. As athletes mature, they are better able to process, follow, and adhere to directions that minimize injury risk. In general, when an external resistance such as a barbell or dumbbell is lifted, the set is performed to muscle failure. Exercises that use body weight as resistance usually have a set number of repetitions as a goal, although sometimes muscle failure occurs before the goal is reached. Depending on the training goal, the load must be individualized and age appropriate. Once you can perform the desired repetitions in a set without reaching muscle failure, increase the resistance by 5 to 10 percent.

Training goals will influence the workout program. Improving local muscle endurance requires high volume (sets of 20 to 25 repetitions) and low intensity. Hypertrophy training acts as the entry point to higher-quality training and requires 10 to 20 repetitions per set and low to moderate intensity. In basic strength training, the intensity is high (80 to 90 percent of capacity), but the volume is low (2 to 5 repetitions per set). Power training, which usually includes explosive movements, requires a higher intensity (90 to 95 percent of capacity) and a low volume (2 to 5 repetitions per set). In general, soccer players should focus on higher-volume exercises of low to moderate intensity, performed twice a week during the season with a focus on maintenance. Save strength and power gains for the off-season.

Safety is key when working out in a weight room. Always work with a spotter. Use safety collars on weights. Lift with your legs, not your back, when picking up weight plates. Drink fluids regularly, and use correct posture and form. Dress properly, and be careful not to drop weights. Consider keeping a workout journal to track your progress. Listen to your body, and don't work through joint pain or unusual muscle pain. See a physician who specializes in sports medicine. If you want to recruit help in the weight room, consult a certified strength and conditioning specialist (CSCS certification) or certified personal trainer (CPT certification).

THE SOCCER PLAYER IN MOTION

Unlike individual sports such as golf, dance, swimming, cycling, and running in which the individual athlete largely dictates her own performance, soccer is a team sport. A team sport adds the dimensions of direct opponents, teammates, a ball, and rules regarding fouls and conduct that are applied during a constantly changing environment of individual, small group, and large group offensive and defensive tactics. A team sport such as soccer requires a range of complexity and intensity and physical and mental preparation beyond what is seen in many individual sports.

Preparation for competition in a team sport involves skill acquisition, tactical development, mental preparation, and physical training. Soccer demands its players to prepare nearly all aspects of physical fitness. As a result, a well-trained soccer player typically is pretty good in all aspects of fitness if not especially outstanding in any one aspect (in many cases, agility). A sprinter must have speed. A marathoner must have endurance. A weightlifter must have strength. Unlike these sports, soccer does not require a player to excel in any one area of fitness to be successful. This explains part of soccer's appeal—anyone can play.

This chapter focuses on the physical demands of soccer, but inherent in any discussion of the physical work required is the inclusion of some basic tactics. Tactics and fitness are intimately related. To know the players, one must know the game. Is a team's tactical performance the result of the players' fitness levels? Or does a higher fitness level allow the team to execute a broader vision of the game? That's soccer's version of the chicken or the egg question.

The Sport of Soccer

At its most basic level, soccer appears to be a game of nonstop motion. The adult game consists of two 45-minute periods that are played with a running clock. (In leagues with younger players, the duration of each half is shorter.) There is no allowance in the rules for the clock to stop. Although the clock runs continuously, the ball is not in play for the full 90 minutes. In general, the ball is in play for only 65 to 70 minutes. All those seconds when the ball is out of play—after a goal, before a corner, during an injury, when a player is singled out by the referee, and so on—add up. If the referee believes these circumstances are shortening the game, additional time, called stoppage time, may be added to the end of each half. One of the charms of the game is that the only person who knows the actual game time is the referee. Note: Some leagues, such as the National Collegiate Athletic Association (NCAA) and many high school leagues, control match time from the sideline and do allow the referee to stop the clock.

Since the game is not continuous, neither is the running of each player. People who study the movement of soccer describe several distinct actions: standing, walking, jogging, cruising, and sprinting. Cruising is defined as running with manifest purpose and effort, which is faster than a jog but slower than a sprint. The speeds above jogging are sometimes further defined as high-intensity running and very high-intensity running, which are further combined with jumping, sideways running, diagonal running, and backward running. A soccer player will execute nearly 1,000 distinct actions during a match. For the player, action changes every four to six seconds. When the running pattern is viewed like this, the game is no longer considered to be continuous activity simply because of a running clock. Instead, soccer is a hybrid of many actions, speeds, and changes of direction. Because the action changes frequently, it is not surprising that soccer players consistently score extremely high on agility.

Successful soccer is about how each team uses space. Soccer tactics can be summarized in a simple concept: When on offense, make the field as big as possible; when on defense, make the field as small as possible.

Ball Movement

The objective of soccer is the same as in any other team sport: Score more than the opponent. On average, 1.5 to 2 goals are scored per match. When counted over many matches, shooting success is pretty low. The overall shots-to-goals ratio is typically 10-to-1. At the 2008 Euro Championship, the average number of passes by a team was 324 per match. Because of the nature of the sport, ball possession changes constantly. Over 90 minutes, a team will have about 240 separate ball possessions. That averages to about 11 seconds per possession. (Remember, your team does not have possession for the full 90 minutes; the other team has possession, too.)

A ball possession can be brief with no completed passes or a long string of completed passes before possession is lost because of poor skill, an intercepted pass, a tackle, a ball lost out of play, or a goal. When plotted over thousands of matches, about 40 percent of all possessions have no completed passes, and 80 to 90 percent of possessions involve four players and three passes or less (figure 1.1). This explains why so many small-sided training activities are 4v4; it is the essence of the game.

If your team gains possession close to your opponent's goal, the number of players and passes will be less. This is an important concept. Forcing your opponent to make a mistake near its own goal puts your team at a distinct advantage. In soccer, goals often are the result of an opponent's mistake instead of a long string of passes by the attacking team. Strange as it sounds, high-pressure defense in the opponent's defensive end is an important offensive tactic. Because soccer is a hybrid of running speeds and directions, it also is a hybrid of possession and quick strike strategies.

In the English Premier League, about 80 percent of any individual player's possessions are only one touch (a redirect) or two touches (control and pass), with no dribbling. Also in the English Premier League, about 70 percent of goals come from one-touch shots, and

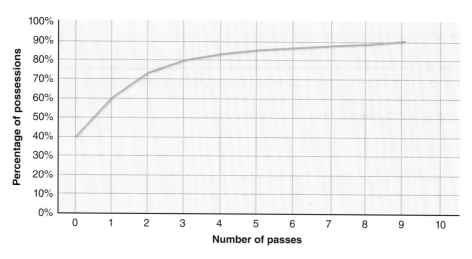

Figure 1.1   Number of passes per possession.

about two-thirds come from open play. The remaining come from restarts—fouls, corners, and penalty kicks (PKs). Combine these stats with the number of passes, and it becomes obvious that soccer is a passing game, not a dribbling game. The less dribbling and the faster passes are played, the faster the game overall.

Physical Demands on the Soccer Player

Many years ago, I asked someone how far a player runs in a soccer match and was told 10 miles. I did the math—10 miles in 90 minutes was 9 minutes per mile; this is doable. But a typical field is 110 yards (100 m) long, and 10 miles is 16,000 meters. That would mean I would have to run the length of the field 145 times at a constant 9-minute-per-mile pace to accumulate 10 miles; this is not likely.

Tracking a player's running distance isn't easy. People have used a paper and pencil coding system (at matches or while watching video replays), step counters, a GPS, and more. No matter what the method, getting the data is labor intensive and time consuming. Those who study the physical demands of soccer generally agree that the average running distance in adult male professional soccer is between 6 and 8.5 miles (9,700 to 13,700 m). Adult female professional soccer players run about 5 miles (8,000 m), but there are reports of female midfielders covering the 6 miles (9,700 m) males run. The total distance decreases in younger players, who play a slower and shorter game.

Since soccer is played at many different paces, the distance is divided according to speed. The general observation is that one-half to two-thirds of the game is played at the slower, more aerobic paces of walking and jogging. The rest is at higher, more anaerobic paces plus sideways and backward running. In addition, distances vary by position. Central attacking and holding midfielders cover the most distance followed by wing midfielders and defenders, strikers, and finally central defenders. Some call the slower paces *positional intensities* (get to the right place on the field) and the faster paces *strategic intensities* (make something happen).

Matches may be won or lost by a strategically timed sprint, so many select teams look carefully for fast, skilled, and tactically savvy players, understanding that endurance can be improved by training. In general, sprints in soccer are 10 to 30 yards (9 to 27 m) long and happen every 45 to 90 seconds. The overall distance an adult male professional player covers at a sprint is 800 to 1,000 yards (730 to 910 m), although in 10- to 30-yard (9 to 27 m) chunks. Hard runs (cruising) happen every 30 to 60 seconds. The time between these hard runs is spent walking, jogging, or standing.

The physiological load on a player when running at any speed is increased by about 15 percent when the player is dribbling a ball. Therefore, one simple way to increase the intensity of any activity is for players to dribble. Small-sided games (4v4 or smaller) that increase the number of ball-contact opportunities usually are more intense than games played in larger groups (8v8 or more) during which ball contact is less frequent and players have more opportunities to stand and walk.

Physiological Demands on the Soccer Player

Many attempts have been made to describe the physiological demands on the soccer player. A basic factor to observe is heart rate during a match. When a person goes for a jog, his heart rate increases rapidly and then settles to a plateau that stays fairly constant throughout the run. When this happens, oxygen demand is being met by oxygen supply. When the jogger stops, the heart rate slows rapidly to a new low recovery plateau that is still above resting heart rate until it finally returns to the resting level. The corresponding oxygen consumption is shown in figure 1.2 (page 4).

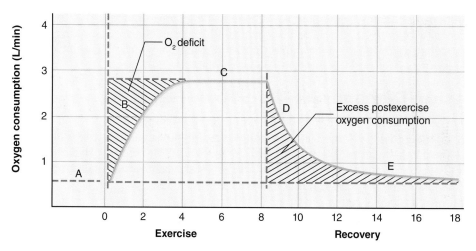

Figure 1.2   Oxygen consumption during exercise and recovery.

In a soccer player, a remarkably similar pattern emerges, and average heart rates are reported (figure 1.3). When the time scale is expanded, however, the pattern is quite different and reflects the intermittent nature of the game. The heart rate is rarely very steady during a match. Brief, rapid increases in response to faster runs are followed by rapid drops in heart rate during recovery periods (figure 1.4). Most reports show the typical heart rate range of a competitive adult soccer player is 150 to 170 beats per minute, with periods at or above 180 beats per minute. Most players work at 75 to 80 percent of capacity. Based on common interpretations of exercise heart rate, soccer is considered an aerobic exercise.

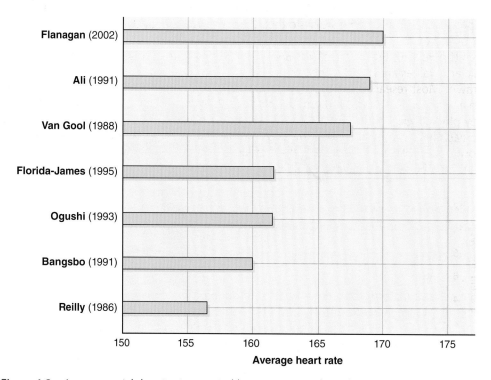

Figure 1.3   Average match heart rate reported by seven research studies.

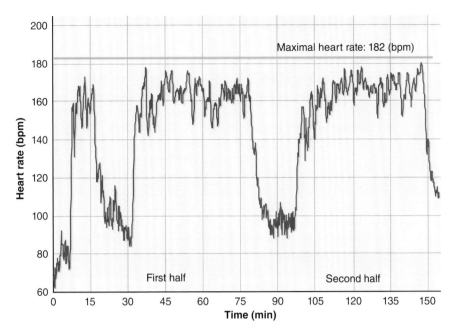

Figure 1.4   Heart rate fluctuations during a soccer match.
Courtesy of Dr. Peter Krustrup.

When the body works intensely, lactic acid is produced. Lactic acid is a product of anaerobic metabolism. Its buildup is perceived as pain (burn) in the exercising muscles, but lactic acid is rapidly removed during recovery. The resting level of lactic acid is around 1 unit. High levels for most people are 6 to 10 units. Anaerobic athletes such as wrestlers and rowers can produce lactic acid levels well into their teens or even 20s. Soccer does not require that kind of anaerobic challenge. Most reports show an elevated level of lactic acid during a match (figure 1.5), but it is hardly overwhelming considering the spectrum seen in sports. Lactic acid values are based on the time between the last intense run and when the blood is drawn. Most researchers sample blood at a fixed time (as seen in figure 1.5). If it has been a while since the last hard run, the blood sample could show a low level of lactic acid. A key physiological feature of a well-trained soccer player is the ability to recover quickly after each hard run, so it is not surprising that lactic acid values in soccer players seem to be low. Soccer players are able to get rid of lactic acid quickly because soccer training has taught their bodies to recover very quickly.

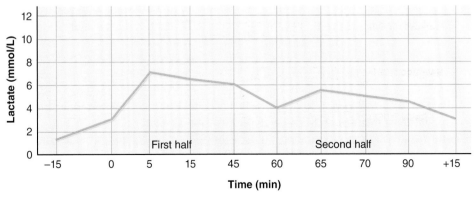

Figure 1.5   Lactic acid levels during a soccer match.
Courtesy of Dr. Peter Krustrup.

Understanding Body Chemistry and Soccer

To understand the demands of soccer, you need to understand the basics of energy. To perform mechanical work, the body needs fuel, which goes through a chemical process to provide energy. A car has one tank that holds one type of fuel, but the body has a number of fuel options found in multiple tanks. Fuel preference depends on fuel availability and the intensity of exercise.

Our bodies need energy, which we obtain from the sun through the ingestion of food. Technically we do not make energy; we transfer energy from the sun through food to the cells so the cells can perform their specific jobs. The currency of cellular work, exercise included, is adenosine triphosphate, or ATP. The adenosine backbone has three phosphates attached. Energy is stored in the chemical "glue" that holds the phosphates to the adenosine molecule. To get the energy, we must strip off a phosphate and release the energy, leaving a two-phosphate molecule called adenosine diphosphate, or ADP. Enzymes accelerate this process. Once the phosphate has been split and the energy released, we need to replenish our ATP warehouse by gathering enough energy to reattach a phosphate to that ADP. The body is constantly using and replenishing ATP. The estimate is that the total amount of ATP in the human body would probably fill something between a shot glass and a juice glass. This is why we have to keep refilling our stores. We are never completely at rest because the body always uses and replenishes ATP.

Released energy is used for many tasks. During exercise, energy is used primarily for muscle contraction, an enormously complex mechanism. The mechanical work of a muscle functions much like a ratchet. Each turn of the ratchet requires energy from a chemical source. Each turn uses energy, so the ratchet needs more energy to keep going.

Only about 40 percent of the energy available is actually used for cellular work, such as muscle contraction. The remainder is released as heat. The rapid breakdown of ATP during exercise to power all those ratchets heats the body. This heat needs to be dissipated so we do not overheat.

Anaerobic Metabolism

The word *anaerobic* means "in the absence of oxygen." We have two ways to produce energy anaerobically. One is simply to break down ATP and release the energy. If more ATP is needed, the body can take two ADPs and slide a phosphate and its energy from one ADP to the other to make a new ATP, turning the donor ADP into adenosine monophosphate, or AMP. Both processes are incredibly fast, but they drain the supply of available ATP almost as quickly. If there were any activity that ran this way exclusively, we would run out of fuel quickly, causing contraction to cease.

Once an ATP has been used, it must be replenished. The body does this by transferring a phosphate and its accompanying energy from another high-energy molecule called phosphocreatine (abbreviated as either PC or CP) to the ADP. This gives us a new ATP and a free creatine that must be resupplied with high energy for bonding a phosphate to be ready for the next transfer. If you were to sprint using only this as a fuel source (which never happens), the sprint might last 10 seconds at best. The simple ATP–PC cycle goes nonstop with each ratcheting of muscle contraction. There must be a continuous feeding of energy and phosphate to keep the cycle running, which is accomplished by the metabolic breakdown of carbohydrates (glucose) and fats (triglycerides) during exercise.

Another anaerobic way to produce ATP for the ATP–PC cycle and provide energy is the chemical breakdown of glycogen, the body's storage form of glucose. Glycogen is a long chain of glucose molecules stored in many places in the body. For our purposes, we will focus on muscle glycogen as the source. Glucose is a six-carbon molecule that is broken down into two three-carbon units. In the process, enough energy is generated to reattach a phosphate to an ADP molecule and make ATP. Actually, four ATP are produced, but the process needs two ATP to run, so the breakdown of a glucose molecule nets two ATP—not much. Because the process has a far greater source of fuel (muscle glycogen) than our juice glass of ATP, it can continue for a longer time, just not as fast and at the cost of lactic acid accumulation. When lactic acid, a product that causes a burning pain in the muscles, is produced faster than the body can get rid of it, the local tissue chemistry is altered. To prevent injury to the muscle cell, the metabolic process is slowed. This is one aspect of fatigue. If you were to sprint using only the anaerobic breakdown of glucose as fuel (again, this never happens), the estimate is that the sprint might last about 45 seconds before the chemical effects of lactic acid would cause the cells to shut down in an attempt to prevent cell damage.

Aerobic Metabolism

The aerobic breakdown of glucose proceeds through the process just described with one twist. In the presence of oxygen, lactic acid is not produced. Instead, the predecessor of lactic acid moves into a circular cycle that spins off carbon dioxide (those six carbons from the original glucose molecule need to go somewhere) and a number of compounds that carry hydrogen (those six carbons of the glucose molecule have hydrogen attached, and they too need to be dealt with). These hydrogen-containing compounds go through a process that transfers the hydrogen down a series of steps to the final acceptor, oxygen. Each oxygen molecule accepts two hydrogen molecules, producing water. During this transfer of hydrogen, enough energy is captured to transfer to an ADP, secure a phosphate, and replenish spent ATP. Depending on the details, the complete metabolism of a single glucose molecule produces 35 to 40 ATP.

But glucose, a carbohydrate, is not the only substance metabolized aerobically. Fat is a rich fuel source for energy. While glucose is a six-carbon molecule, a triglyceride has a glycerol head (with its three carbons and associated hydrogen) and three fatty acid chains, any of which can be less than 10 to 20 or more carbons in length. In fat metabolism, each fatty acid chain is cut up into two-carbon segments that each follow an aerobic path similar to the one taken by glucose to produce energy. Remember that a glucose molecule is split in half, and each half goes through the energy production process. A triglyceride, on the other hand, is far larger because of its three long fatty acid chains. If each of the three chains has 18 carbons and the process proceeds in two-carbon units (and do not forget the glycerol head), well, you can see the aerobic breakdown of a triglyceride produces far more ATP than does glucose, perhaps by a factor of 10 or more, with the same easily eliminated products of carbon dioxide and water. The problem is that fat metabolism is the slowest process.

We also can produce energy from the aerobic metabolism of proteins, but the amount of energy we get from proteins during exercise is pretty small. Most people tend to ignore the energy contributions of proteins to exercise.

The end products of the aerobic metabolism of carbohydrate and fat are water and carbon dioxide, both easily eliminated, especially when compared to lactic acid. In terms of the time needed to produce ATP, the aerobic breakdown of glucose and fat takes longer than the anaerobic metabolism of glucose and far longer than the ATP–PC cycle. Although speed of production is not its strong point, aerobic metabolism has the capability to produce energy for exercise for an indefinite period of time because everyone has an ample supply of fat.

Energy During Exercise

The interaction of all these metabolic processes can be complicated. At no time is any one of the metabolic processes or sources of fuel supplying 100 percent of the energy needed for exercise. The intensity and duration of the exercise dictates the predominant energy process and fuel. Intensity and duration of exercise are inversely related: The longer the exercise, the lower the intensity; shorter work is more intense. You could not run a marathon at your 100-meter pace, and you would not want to run a 100-meter race at your marathon pace.

Figure 1.6 helps explain this interaction. The X-axis is exercise time, and the Y-axis is the percentage of energy supplied by the various fuel sources. For exercise of very short duration, such as a 40-meter sprint, the primary fuel source is stored ATP and phosphocreatine, but a small portion of energy comes from anaerobic and aerobic metabolism of glucose. As the duration of exercise increases, up to around four minutes, the primary source of energy comes from anaerobic metabolism of glucose, but some energy comes from other pathways. Exercise that lasts four minutes or more is fueled primarily by aerobic metabolism of glucose and fat, with a progressively smaller fraction of energy coming from the other processes.

The amount of energy available from stored ATP and phosphocreatine is very small. The amount of energy from stored carbohydrate is greater but still limited. The amount of available fuel from fat is essentially unlimited. The fat that is stored within the muscle, that surrounds the organs, and that lies under the skin is far more than anyone would need for exercise. But remember, it takes time to obtain fuel from fat. It is estimated that if fat were the sole source of fuel for running, you could run at only about 50 percent of capacity—a walk or slow jog at best. Muscle glycogen also is a limited fuel source. Someone who runs out of glycogen will slow down because the main source of fuel is now from fat. Most people run out of muscle glycogen in the fibers recruited for exercise in about 90 minutes. Soccer players can therefore run out of glycogen during a match. To compensate, soccer players should follow the dietary recommendations to increase muscle glycogen that individual-sport athletes have wisely adopted. A combination of training and high carbohydrate intake allows the muscle to pack in more glycogen, allowing the player to go further into the match before running out.

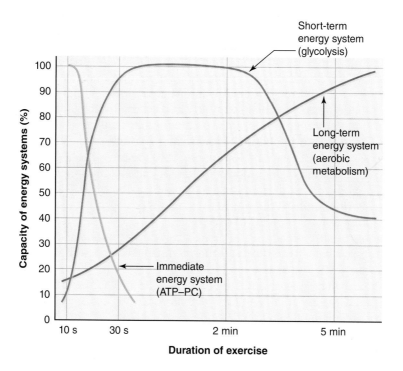

Figure 1.6   Relationship of exercise duration and energy systems.

Application to Soccer

Let's get back to the game. Remember, soccer is a game of numerous short sprints and episodes of high-intensity anaerobic work separated by periods of low-intensity aerobic recovery in preparation for the next bout of high-intensity work. During a sprint, shot, jump, tackle, or cut, some ATP is spent and some glucose is used to power the muscles for the hard work. Then the player recovers during a lower-intensity phase of play (walking, jogging, standing) during which ATP is replenished and lactic acid is removed. (Lactic acid is metabolized aerobically, which is one reason you breathe hard after slowing down or stopping.) This prepares the muscles for the next bout of hard work.

How long before the player is ready to work hard again depends on how quickly ATP is replenished, how much lactic acid is removed, and how a few other electrochemical processes connected with contraction are completed. What you need to understand is that the important parts of the game—the parts that define who wins, those high-intensity runs—are fueled primarily by anaerobic means, and the recovery periods are accomplished aerobically.

Recovery is an aerobic event. This is something most coaches and players either forget or ignore. The higher the player's aerobic capacity, the faster she will recover and the more frequently she can work hard, going deeper into the match before tiring. A player with poor aerobic fitness will take longer to recover from a sprint before again being able to use that blazing speed, and chances are each successive sprint will be shorter and slower. Research shows that training-induced improvements in speed are not nearly as great as training-induced improvements in endurance. That is why speed is such a highly valued trait in a soccer player, because the coach knows endurance can be improved more easily than speed. Coaches look for fast players who can improve their endurance instead of players who can run all day but need to improve speed. Yet the modern game is not about raw speed. It is about how fast a player recovers to use the speed she has over and over.

Some studies can nearly rank the final standings of a league's clubs according to each team's aerobic capacity. Aerobic capacity for rapid recovery is that important. Coaches are very adept at designing training sessions to improve endurance and the ability to recover. To raise intensity, they use short small-sided games on a small field, with restrictions to force play (for example, multiple two-minute games with limited recovery between each game; 4v4 or fewer for more ball contacts; or games in a penalty area or smaller marked area to force quick decisions, with restrictions such as overlapping every pass with a sprint). The smaller sides mean less downtime, so the body has to learn to adapt for fast recovery from the temporary fatigue induced by each sprint. For endurance, activities usually involve more players in a larger space, with restrictions that force a more constant pace of play for a longer period of time (for example, a 15- to 20-minute drill or games of 8v8 or more, in a three-quarter or full field, with restrictions such as all players in the attacking zone before a shot). A player with higher aerobic fitness can recover more quickly than an unfit player. The fit player gets to a new position faster and is ready for higher-intensity work well before the unfit player.

Jogging at a constant pace around a field or a park will improve jogging ability, but it won't train the body to do what is necessary to recover in a start–stop game. When jogging, you recover once—at the end. In soccer, recovery happens repeatedly. A well-trained soccer player will be able to keep the heads of each ratchet in the muscle well supplied with ATP to keep the ATP–PC process running and delay the influence of lactic acid on local muscle fatigue. Players who are unable to rapidly replenish the ATP for that ATP–PC cycle will be standing around waiting while other players are running past.

Muscle Fiber Recruitment

You may have heard of fast-twitch and slow-twitch muscle fibers. We are all blessed with a mosaic of muscle fibers with unique characteristics that make us supremely adaptable to a multitude of activities. Basically, the big fast-twitch fibers produce a lot of tension very quickly but can't keep producing this amount of tension for many contractions. The smaller slow-twitch fibers produce less tension at a slower rate but can keep contracting repeatedly. Think back to the description of energy, and apply that to the concept of fiber type. Fast-twitch fibers produce most of their energy anaerobically (for a rapid production of tension), while slow-twitch fibers produce most of their energy aerobically (for repeated contractions). The distribution of fast-twitch and slow-twitch fibers is, for the most part, fixed by genetics. Although some people might reason that a soccer player should have more of one type than the other, most studies show a soccer player has about a 50:50 ratio. Remember, soccer is the game of the masses, so it makes sense that no genetically predetermined factor, such as a high percentage of slow-twitch fibers in a marathoner or height in basketball, is a requirement to play the game.

Female Players

Much of the worldwide growth in soccer is due to the increased participation of women. Although the rules are the same, there are subtle tactical differences between the men's and the women's games that may not be evident to casual fans. The general pattern of work is similar but at a lower running volume and pace, although some female midfielders cover the 6 miles (9,700 m) male players do. Women have physiological differences such as a lower engine capacity. This lower capacity of females is the result of less muscle mass, smaller hearts, less total blood volume, and less hemoglobin. A female playing a match of the same duration and field size as a male and running the same distance as a male will have to play the game at a higher intensity. It isn't unusual for adult female professional players to exhibit heart rates above those of their male counterparts. They work hard.

Female athletes have other issues that can cause health problems. The female athlete triad is the interaction of disordered eating, menstrual dysfunction, and reduced bone density. Some female athletes choose not to eat appropriately, which can lead to a disruption of normal hormonal balance evident in menstrual problems. A disruption of normal hormonal balance, especially of estrogen, can reduce bone density. The repeated impact of physical training can then lead to stress fractures, mostly in the lower extremities. Because the triad begins with reduced calorie intake and possibly disordered eating, ensuring females are consuming adequate calories is imperative for maintaining normal menstrual function and healthy bones.

Females also need to ingest appropriate amounts of iron and calcium. Even athletes on a vegetarian diet can get plenty of these minerals with proper food selection. The Fédération Internationale de Football Association (FIFA) has produced an excellent booklet on the female player; see the additional resources on page 207.

Nutrition and Hydration

Our fuel for exercise comes from the food we eat. We all have plenty of fat, but carbohydrate storage capacity is limited, meaning we have to refuel carbohydrates frequently. For you to be a player in motion, you need to be well fueled, and that comes from carbohydrates. FIFA has an excellent booklet on nutrition specifically written for the nonscientific audience. See the additional resources on page 207.

Dehydration is a problem in soccer. The length of the game, the intensity of the running, the elements, and the lack of planned stoppages all contribute to players not getting necessary fluid during a match. A fluid deficit of as little as 2 percent—only 3 pounds (1.4 kg) of fluid loss in a 150-pound (68 kg) player—can negatively affect performance.

Players should take advantage of normal stoppages to drink water, sports drinks, or both. To keep fluids available, players place water bottles in or around the goal and along the touchlines and drink during injury stoppages or other dead-ball situations. Because central midfielders are the farthest from the field boundaries, they have the most difficulty taking advantage of stoppages, so they need to make a conscious effort to get to water wherever it is placed, and the coach needs to make sure that fluids get to them during such stoppages.

Players who produce very salty sweat might be inclined to choose a drink with salt and add extra salt to their meals. These players can be identified as those whose shirts show a crusty substance as the water in their sweat evaporates from their clothing. This is especially obvious when they wear dark shirts.

The other problem with soccer players is that they tend to not drink enough between training sessions or matches. There are reports that as many as 40 percent of players on a team could be clinically dehydrated even before they step onto the field.

The typical formula for fluid replacement is 1.5 pints (24 oz or 720 ml) of fluid per pound (.5 kg) of body weight lost, so know your weight and check it often. Full replenishment cannot be done in one sitting. It can take a full day. Keep a close eye on your urine color. If it looks like dilute lemonade, you are probably OK. But if it looks more like apple juice, you need to drink more fluids. See the nutrition booklet in the additional resources (page 207) for more information.

Drugs and Food Supplements

We cannot seem to separate sports from drugs, especially so-called performance-enhancing drugs, or PEDs. Although drugs seem to be endemic in sports such as cycling, soccer has little history of drug abuse. This is probably because soccer does not rely on one specific factor that could be enhanced by a PED to affect the outcome, as anabolic steroids do for weightlifters or erythropoietin (EPO) does for road cyclists. FIFA's own statistics show a trivial number of positive drug tests, and half of those positive tests were for recreational drugs, not PEDs.

A high percentage of athletes take over-the-counter, and largely unnecessary, supplements. Some reports show nearly 100 percent of Olympic athletes in some sports from certain countries take supplements. The most common supplement is a multivitamin, but that is not the point. The supplement industry does not follow the same purity rules that the FDA requires for the food and drug industries. Therefore, what is on the label may not be a full accounting of what is actually in the bottle.

Recently, the International Olympic Committee (IOC) went to some supplement stores and randomly selected supplements known to be used by athletes. The IOC tested the products and found that nearly one-quarter of them would have produced a positive drug test. In sports, the athlete is always responsible for a positive drug test. Any player who thinks college, international, or professional play is in his future will face drug testing and must be very careful about what he ingests.

If you eat a well-rounded diet, choosing from a wide variety of fresh and colorful items from all food groups, supplements will only enrich your urine and empty your wallet. The renowned sports supplement researcher Dr. Ron Maughan from Loughborough University (UK) has an axiom: "If it works, it is probably banned. If it is not banned, it probably doesn't work." Why take the chance?

Injury Prevention

Injuries are a part of all sports. The most common soccer injury is a contusion (bruise) when you get kicked, fall, or bumped. The most common location is the lower extremity, mostly between the knee and ankle. Most leg contusions do not cause a player to miss much training time or competition. The top four time-loss soccer injuries are ankle sprains, knee sprains, hamstring strains, and groin strains. In elite soccer, hamstring strains are most common. At lower levels of play, ankle sprains are number one.

There are some gender differences. Females have a higher rate of injury to the anterior cruciate ligament of the knee. Newer data suggest that females suffer more concussions than do males. The difference in concussion rates may be real, or it could be skewed because women tend to be more forthcoming than men about head injuries.

Good prevention programs, when substituted for a traditional warm-up, have been shown to reduce common injuries by about one-third. FIFA presents an excellent graduated warm-up (The 11+) that is the subject of chapter 2. For players and teams with a special concern about hamstring strains, pay close attention to the hamstrings exercise and the balance exercises. These have been shown to reduce hamstring strains. The key to any injury prevention program is compliance. Programs such as The 11+ are not an occasional diversion. Players must complete these programs at every training session and do a shorter version before competition.

Heat Illnesses

For many countries in the northern hemisphere, soccer is a fall to spring sport; summer is the off-season. In the United States, the professional game parallels the baseball season, making it a spring to fall sport. Depending on the time of year, soccer in the southern states can be played in pretty oppressive conditions. All summer leagues and tournaments need to have a plan in place to handle players suffering from heat illnesses. Players who succumb to the heat may initially show minor symptoms such as heat cramps, but problems can rapidly progress to far more serious issues such as heat exhaustion and heatstroke, which is a potentially fatal collapse of the body's ability to control its temperature. You may have read about heat-related deaths in American football players.

The body loses heat by radiation through radiant loss of heat through heat waves; convection (like standing in front of a fan or air conditioner); conduction, which is direct contact with a cooler surface (like placing an ice-cold towel on the head); or evaporation, which is the most important mechanism during exercise. Sweat production is not the loss of heat; the evaporation of the sweat results in heat loss. Any barrier to heat loss will slow the rate of evaporation. Two barriers frequently encountered in soccer include clothing, especially dark clothing that covers much of the body, and humidity. Today's sports clothing is designed to aid evaporation.

Whenever matches are scheduled during hot and humid weather, put strategies in place for making fluids available. Many youth leagues, particularly in the south, have water breaks in each half as part of the rules. If water breaks are not part of the rules, the coaches can approach the referee and ask for a break if the conditions warrant it. The referee has this authority and would probably appreciate the break as well. During the men's gold medal match at the Beijing Olympics, a water break was included in each half because of the conditions.

Fatigue

A good definition of fatigue is the failure to maintain an expected power output—you want to run fast but are unable to. Fatigue can be both general and temporary and can come from a number of mechanisms. For example, to run fast, you need muscle glycogen. When muscle glycogen levels decline below set levels, you walk. Increasing muscle glycogen stores through training and proper food selection will delay fatigue and allow you to go deeper into the match before tiring. In addition, an ample store of glucose ensures that the brain has a ready supply of the only fuel it can use. The brain can become fatigued, too. Elevated body temperature and the accompanying loss of fluids by evaporation are also factors in general fatigue. Because body temperature affects performance, it is necessary to keep fluid levels up so the body can produce sweat for evaporation and heat loss. Drink often.

Temporary fatigue is a result of rapidly altered and remedied local muscle chemistry that affects the ability of the muscle fibers to contract. Lactic acid contributes to temporary fatigue. After a few repeated fast runs, you tire, but in a few minutes you can be back and ready to go again. Any improvement in aerobic capacity will let you do more, or longer, hard runs before temporary fatigue sets in by improving your ability to recover more quickly. Training for rapid recovery minimizes the effects of temporary fatigue by speeding up the removal of lactic acid and the recovery of processes that couple the processes associated with excitation of the muscle with the muscle's ability to contract.

THE FIFA WARM-UP

The Fédération Internationale de Football Association (FIFA) is the world governing body for soccer. At the 1994 FIFA World Cup, a high-level FIFA administrator casually asked the question, "Can't we make the game safer?" Everyone has to accept that participation in sport, especially a contact sport, is risky. Players will get injured. But can't steps be taken to lessen the rate of injury?

That simple question became the impetus for the development of the FIFA Medical Assessment and Research Centre (F-MARC). One of F-MARC's primary goals was to reduce the incidence and severity of injuries in soccer. Their first task was to document the true incidence of injury at the world championship level. F-MARC needed to know what injuries to try to prevent. Should they attack the most severe injuries, those that result in the greatest loss of time? Or the most common injuries, those that affect the most players? Many injury studies already existed, but the methods used were inconsistent, making comparisons and conclusions nearly impossible. F-MARC took the best methods available and started an injury surveillance program, beginning with the 1998 FIFA World Cup, that continues today at all FIFA-sponsored tournaments. This gives F-MARC a stable database on injuries at the world championship level.

When F-MARC was organized, most prevention reports were based not on research evidence but on expert opinion. Before the mid-1990s, only one experimental research project designed to prevent injury in soccer—a study out of Sweden—had been published. But that program was so extensive that it was hard to zero in on the most effective aspects to relate to the local coach.

Injury prevention research is a four-step process. First, determine which injuries should be prevented through an injury surveillance program. Second, determine the mechanism of injury (how the injuries happen). Third, devise prevention protocols. Finally, implement the protocols on a large group of players and see if the injury rate decreases. In practice, a large group of players is recruited and randomly divided into two groups. One group receives the intervention, and one group does not. All injuries are recorded over a specific period of time, and the injury rates of the two groups are compared.

That first Swedish study reported a dramatic 75 percent reduction in all injuries, but in reality, no one could comply with the number of interventions or provide the personnel required to carry out their extremely rigid program. The first F-MARC injury prevention program, conducted on mostly high-school-age European boys, showed a one-third reduction in overall injury rate, which is a level of reduction that seems to be consistent with subsequent studies. That program was the pilot for F-MARC's initial prevention program called The 11, which consisted of 10 prevention exercises and the call for fair play. (At the world championship level, nearly half the injuries to men and about one-quarter to one-third of all injuries to women are due to foul play.)

An important aspect of injury prevention is establishing the risk factors of a particular injury. Risk factors are classified as player-related factors (lack of skill, poor fitness, prior injury) or non-player-related factors (quality of refereeing, field conditions, environment). Some risk factors, such as fitness level and lack of skill, are modifiable, while others, such as gender, age, environment, and field quality, are not. Research suggests that interventions are successful at preventing injury for some modifiable factors (e.g., hamstring strength). But it is important to remember that the number one predictor of an injury is a history of that injury. A player who has had a strained hamstring has a dramatically higher risk of getting the same injury; some reports suggest the risk is increased by a factor of eight times. The obvious conclusion, then, is to prevent the first injury.

Since the original Swedish project, a number of prevention trials have been conducted and published in medical literature. Some of the trials were general and designed to lower the overall injury rate. Other trials attempted to prevent specific injuries. For example, in team sports, programs were designed specifically to prevent ankle sprains, knee sprains, hamstring strains, and groin strains. Prevention programs may be classified as primary prevention (prevent the first injury occurrence) or secondary prevention (prevent a recurrent injury). Programs that prevent hamstring strains and knee sprains are considered primary prevention but are still effective in secondary prevention, while programs that prevent ankle sprains are considered secondary prevention. To date, no prevention program has been able to prevent an athlete's first ankle sprain.

Preventing injury to the knee, particularly to the anterior cruciate ligament (ACL), has been studied intensely. ACL injuries in sports such as soccer and basketball occur at a higher rate in females than in males by a factor of three to eight times. This is a particular problem for girls in middle school and high school, but it extends into college as well. It is not uncommon for a female soccer player to have multiple ACL injuries; the younger the player when the first injury occurs, the greater the risk of another injury. A number of prevention studies have been conducted; some yielded impressive results (up to a 70 percent reduction in ACL injuries in female youth players), while others failed to show any reduction.

The key to any prevention program is compliance. These programs are quite effective when they are part of the regular warm-up for training and competition. When performed regularly, a prevention program can reduce ACL injury rates. When the prevention program is performed only sporadically, all bets are off. Most experts want to see compliance rates of 75 percent or higher.

Hamstring strains have become a huge problem in high-caliber competition. The increase in pace of the modern game has pushed hamstring strains from an insignificant injury 20 years ago to one of the top four injuries in professional soccer, sometimes the number one injury on a club. For a professional club to see six hamstring strains or more in a season is not unusual. But research shows that hamstring strains can be prevented, both the first strain as well as recurrent strains. When done regularly, the hamstrings exercise on page 30 has been shown to be extremely effective at preventing hamstring strain injury.

Groin strains are a particular problem in soccer and in ice hockey. Players typically perform static stretching to prevent groin strains. The problem is that there is no consensus on the effectiveness of preexercise static stretching in preventing injury in general, much less a specific injury such as a groin strain. The shift from static stretching to dynamic stretching has been shown to have some success at injury prevention. Static stretching is fine, but most experts suggest it be done on another day away from the performance of the sport or during the cool-down, not as part of the preactivity warm-up.

A groin strain is not the same as the sports hernia common in ice hockey and soccer. A *groin strain* is a typical pulled muscle, usually an injury to the adductor longus muscle. Most players can identify the exact moment the injury occurred. A *sports hernia*, also known as Gilmore's groin, athletic pubalgia, or athlete's hernia) is an inflammation or tear of connective tissue (not an injury to the muscles of the lower abdomen) near the location of a traditional hernia. A specific instance that caused the injury cannot be recalled. The player will complain of groin pain when sprinting or during powerful kicking. In the doctor's office, the pain can sometimes be reproduced during seated or lying resisted hip flexion or while coughing. Although a vast majority of these injuries occur in males, the sports hernia can also happen to females. The exact cause is unknown, and diagnosing this injury is a clinical challenge for the physician because so many other problems can mimic the pain.

Unfortunately, there is no definitive diagnostic test or any method of imaging that is specific for a sports hernia. Ice hockey has a prevention program for this hernia that seems to be effective, but when a modification was tried in professional soccer players, the results were inconclusive, probably due to poor compliance by the players and teams. An athlete with chronic groin pain should see a sports medicine specialist because of the difficulty in making an accurate diagnosis. Rest, massage, strengthening, medication, and more have all been suggested, but the pain frequently returns. A routine hernia repair, done more frequently in Europe than in the United States, has been shown to be a reasonably effective surgical intervention, but it may not be the solution for everyone.

As the evidence began to accumulate, F-MARC developed the second version of The 11. In the revision, the exercises were progressive, and the entire program was substituted for the typical generalized warm-up a team might do before training or a match. The result was The 11+. The 11+ was tested on female youths in Norway, with two great results. First, they showed the expected overall injury reduction of about one-third. Second, they had excellent compliance to the program because its revised design increased the interest of and participation by players and coaches. As a warm-up, The 11+ prepares players for training and competition. As a teaching tool, a number of the exercises teach players the proper techniques for landing, cutting, and pivoting. When the landing is done properly, the knee should flex over the planted foot (figure 2.1a) and not be allowed to collapse into what is called a valgus position (figure 2.1b). The coach needs to watch players do these exercises and correct players who display incorrect landing and cutting techniques.

Although a number of prevention programs are available, The 11+ has gained wide acceptance, and its use continues to grow. Because of its success and specific focus on soccer, the exercises of The 11+ have been used as the foundation for the warm-up in this chapter. (See table 2.1 on page 18.) Additional information about The 11+, including a chart that shows the entire routine, can be found at http://f-marc.com/11plus/index.html. Once a team has learned the exercise routine, the entire program can be completed in 15 to 20 minutes. Remember, The 11+ replaces a team's warm-up.

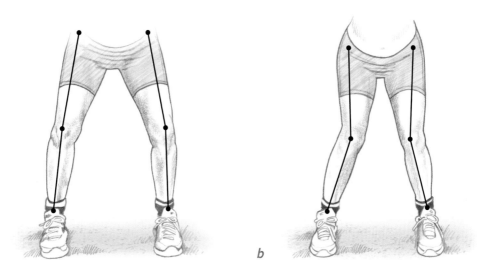

a   b

Figure 2.1   Landing knee position: *(a)* correct; *(b)* incorrect.

Table 2.1 The 11+ Warm-Up Routine

JOGGING EXERCISES

Exercise number	Exercise title	Page number	Sets
1	Jogging straight ahead	20	2
2	Jogging with hip out	21	2
3	Jogging with hip in	22	2
4	Jogging around partner	23	2
5	Jogging and jumping with shoulder contact	24	2
6	Jogging forward and backward	25	2

STRENGTH, PLYOMETRIC, AND BALANCE EXERCISES

Exercise number	Level 1	Level 2	Level 3	Page number	Sets
7	Static bench	Bench with alternating legs	Bench with one-leg lift and hold	26	2; 2 each leg for bench with one-leg lift and hold
8	Static sideways bench	Sideways bench with hip lift	Sideways bench with leg lift	28	2 each side
9	Beginner hamstrings	Intermediate hamstrings	Advanced hamstrings	30	1
10	Single-leg stance with ball hold	Single-leg stance with ball throw to partner	Single-leg stance with partner test	32	2 each leg
11	Squat with toe raise	Walking lunge	One-leg squat	34	2; 2 each leg for one-leg squat
12	Vertical jump	Lateral jump	Box jump	36	2

RUNNING EXERCISES

Exercise number	Exercise title	Page number	Sets
13	Running across the pitch	38	2
14	Bounding	39	2
15	Plant and cut	40	2

Adapted from The 11+, developed by F-MARC.

Three Parts of the FIFA Warm-Up

A warm-up gradually prepares the body for more intense exercise, which is important since the body operates more efficiently when warmer than when at resting temperature. For that reason, The 11+ begins with a short period of jogging.

After the jogging exercises, players move into strength, plyometric, and balance exercises. These exercises dynamically stretch the muscles and prepare them for more explosive maneuvers on the pitch.

One of the purposes of a generalized warm-up is to prepare the body for the upcoming activity. Many of the exercises in The 11+ are challenging but not very intense. Each running exercise is performed at a higher intensity, bringing the body closer to the intensity of more formal training. The pace of this running is not sprinting but a fairly hard stride. Increasing running speed means increasing stride rate and increasing stride length. Thus, the movement of the swing leg occurs faster, and the push-off by the ground leg is stronger. The actual muscles used at the various running speeds remain about the same, but the brain tells each active muscle to work harder by recruiting a greater number of muscle cells as well as by asking each cell to contract harder.

Jogging Straight Ahead

Execution

Place 6 to 10 pairs of cones in parallel lines 5 to 10 yards (5 to 9 m) apart—closer for younger players, farther for older players. (This cone configuration will be used for all of the jogging exercises.) If many players are participating, consider setting up two or more sets of parallel cones. Start with a partner from the first pair of cones. Jog with your partner to the last pair of cones. On the way back to the start, progressively increase your speed. Perform this twice.

Muscles Involved

Primary: Hip flexors (psoas major and minor, iliacus), quadriceps (vastus medialis, vastus lateralis, vastus intermedius, rectus femoris), gastrocnemius, soleus

Secondary: Hamstrings (biceps femoris, semitendinosus, semimembranosus), peroneals (peroneus longus, brevis, and tertius), tibialis anterior

Soccer Focus

One purpose of a warm-up is to raise your internal body temperature. This is important because the metabolic functions described in chapter 1 work most efficiently at temperatures above rest. Some general jogging is a simple way to start raising your internal temperature. When you break into a sweat, your internal temperature is well on the way to a range where energy metabolism is most efficient. The 11+ will effectively raise your internal temperature.

Jogging With Hip Out

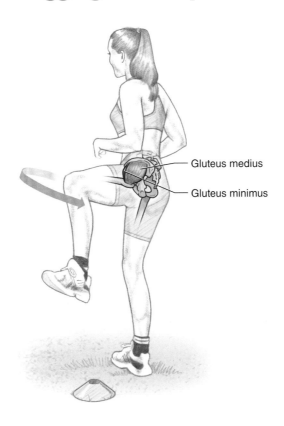

Gluteus medius

Gluteus minimus

Execution

Set up cones in the same configuration as for the jogging straight ahead exercise on the previous page. Walk or jog easily with a partner, stopping at each pair of cones to lift your knee and rotate your hip out. Alternate left and right legs at successive cones. Jog back to the start after the last cone. Perform two sets.

Muscles Involved

Primary: Hip flexors, gluteals (gluteus maximus, medius, and minimus), tensor fasciae latae

Secondary: Adductor longus, adductor magnus (posterior fibers), sartorius, piriformis

Soccer Focus

Many coaches and athletes believe static stretching will improve performance and prevent injury, but the scientific evidence shows otherwise. Dynamic stretching, which involves taking the joint through a full range of motion, does not hamper performance and has been shown to reduce strain injuries. Soccer players are prone to groin injuries and may need to perform specific dynamic stretching of the groin as a part of every warm-up.

Jogging With Hip In

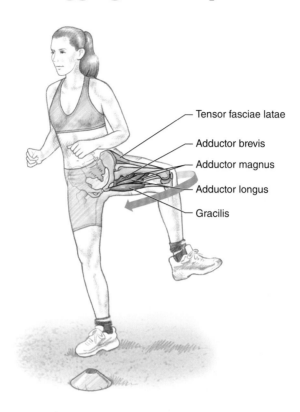

Tensor fasciae latae
Adductor brevis
Adductor magnus
Adductor longus
Gracilis

Execution

Set up cones in the same configuration as for the jogging straight ahead exercise (page 20). Walk or jog easily with a partner, stopping at each pair of cones to lift your knee up and out to the side before rotating your hip inward. Alternate between left and right legs at successive cones. Jog back to the start after the last cone. Perform two sets.

Muscles Involved

Primary: Adductors (adductor longus, adductor magnus, adductor brevis, gracilis) gluteus minimus, gluteus medius

Secondary: Pectineus, tensor fasciae latae

Soccer Focus

Most flexibility programs emphasize opposing muscle groups. This dynamic internal rotation exercise balances out the previous dynamic external rotation exercise. With both of these dynamic flexibility exercises, be sure to move the thigh through the entire range of motion by either ending or beginning at the extremes of motion. These are effective exercises when each rotation attempts to go just a little bit farther.

Jogging Around Partner

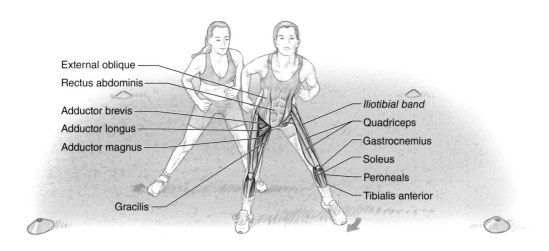

External oblique
Rectus abdominis
Adductor brevis
Adductor longus
Adductor magnus
Gracilis
Iliotibial band
Quadriceps
Gastrocnemius
Soleus
Peroneals
Tibialis anterior

Execution

Set up cones in the same configuration as for the jogging straight ahead exercise (page 20). With a partner, jog together to the first set of cones. Shuffle sideways to meet in the middle. Shuffle an entire circle around your partner as she circles around you, and then return to the cones. Repeat for each pair of cones. Stay on your toes, and keep your center of gravity low by bending your hips and knees. Jog back to the start after the last cone. Perform two sets.

Muscles Involved

Primary: Gastrocnemius, soleus, gluteus maximus, iliotibial band (push-off leg), adductors (pulling leg)

Secondary: Hamstrings, quadriceps, peroneals, tibialis anterior, abdominal core (external oblique, internal oblique, transversus abdominis, rectus abdominis) and spinal extensors (erector spinae, multifidus) for postural control

Soccer Focus

Soccer requires many lateral movements of varying distances, directions, and speeds. Lateral movement is one aspect of agility, which is a prized trait that soccer players are known for. This gentle exercise prepares players for the next exercise. Going both directions balances the load across the legs. As with all exercises that involve movement, be sure your knees don't collapse in.

Jogging and Jumping With Shoulder Contact

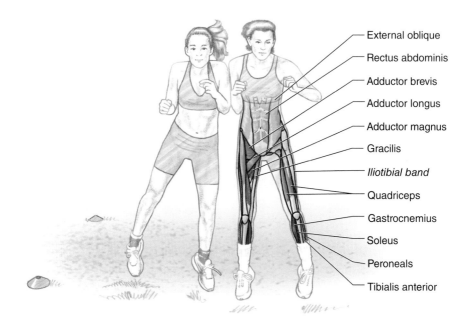

- External oblique
- Rectus abdominis
- Adductor brevis
- Adductor longus
- Adductor magnus
- Gracilis
- *Iliotibial band*
- Quadriceps
- Gastrocnemius
- Soleus
- Peroneals
- Tibialis anterior

Execution

Set up cones in the same configuration as for the jogging straight ahead exercise (page 20). With a partner, jog together to the first pair of cones. Shuffle sideways to meet your partner in the middle, and then jump sideways toward your partner to make shoulder-to-shoulder contact. Land on both feet with your hips and knees bent. Do not let your knees buckle in. Synchronize the timing of your jump and landing with your partner. Repeat at each cone. Jog back to the start after the last cone. Perform two sets.

Muscles Involved

Primary: Gastrocnemius, soleus, gluteus maximus, iliotibial band (push-off leg), adductors (pulling leg), quadriceps, hamstrings

Secondary: Abdominal core, peroneals, tibialis anterior

Soccer Focus

A key factor in knee injuries, especially injuries to the ACL, is the knee collapsing in when the player lands erect. This awkward position adds strain on the ACL that may be sufficient to tear the ligament and damage the meniscus. Many of the exercises in The 11+ teach players to control landing and cutting. This is especially important for female players from middle school age and up, the prime ages for an ACL tear. Land softly and quietly. Be sure your knees don't collapse in.

Jogging Forward and Backward

Execution

Set up cones in the same configuration as for the jogging straight ahead exercise (page 20). With a partner, jog quickly to the second set of cones, and then backpedal quickly to the first set of cones, keeping your hips and knees slightly bent. Jog to the third set of cones and backpedal to the second set of cones. Repeat through all sets of cones. Jog back to the start after the last cone. Take small, quick steps. Perform two sets.

Muscles Involved

Primary: Hip flexors, quadriceps, hamstrings, gastrocnemius, soleus, gluteals

Secondary: Abdominal core, spinal extensors

Soccer Focus

This exercise is done more quickly than the others in this group. Plant your front foot firmly, ensuring the knee stays over the foot and does not buckle in. Jog one cone forward and backward quickly, keeping good balance and posture. Plant the push-off leg firmly, and jog two cones forward quickly. Take small, quick steps, not loping strides. Maintain proper posture—flexed hips and knees—and an almost exaggerated arm action.

Bench

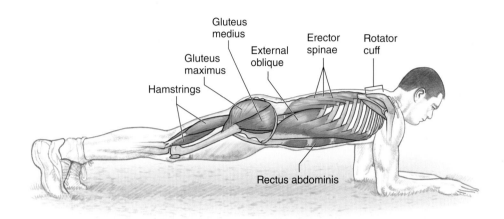

Level 1: static bench.

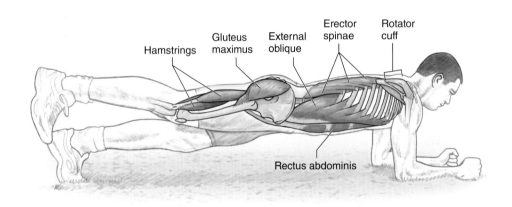

Level 2: bench with alternating legs.

Level 1: Static Bench

Lie on your front, supporting yourself on your forearms and feet. Your elbows should be directly under your shoulders. Lift your body, supporting your weight on your forearms. Pull in your abdomen, and hold the position for 20 to 30 seconds. When this static position is held long enough, you will feel it throughout the core muscles. Proper form is important, so make sure the elbows are directly under the shoulders and your body is in a straight line from the back of the head down to the trunk, hips, and heels. Try not to sway or arch your back. Lower your body to the ground and repeat.

Level 2: Bench With Alternating Legs

Adding a hip extension is a simple way to make this basic core strengthening exercise more difficult. The challenge is to maintain a straight line all the way down the body. Good posture is critical. Lie on your front, supporting yourself on your forearms and feet. Your elbows should be directly under your shoulders. Lift your body, supporting your weight on your forearms. Pull in your abdomen. Lift your right leg and hold for 2 seconds. Lower your right leg, and then lift your left leg, holding for 2 seconds. Continue, alternating legs, for 40 to 60 seconds. For the best results, slowly raise and lower the leg. Keep your body in a straight line. Try not to sway or arch your back. Repeat this exercise for a second 40- to 60-second set.

Level 3: Bench With One-Leg Lift and Hold

This more difficult version of the bench combines isometrics (holding the leg in the up position) with dynamic movement (raising and lowering the leg). Holding the leg up for 20 to 30 seconds adds an additional challenge for the spine and hip extensors. Lie on your front, supporting yourself on your forearms and feet. Your elbows should be directly under your shoulders. Lift your body, supporting your weight on your forearms. Pull in your abdomen. Lift one leg about 6 inches (15 cm) off the ground, and hold the position for 20 to 30 seconds. Keep your body straight. Do not let your opposite hip dip down, and do not sway or arch your lower back. Lower the leg, take a short break, switch legs, and repeat. Do this twice for each leg.

Muscles Involved

Primary: Abdominal core, spinal extensors, gluteals, hamstrings

Secondary: Shoulder stabilizers including rotator cuff (supraspinatus, infraspinatus, subscapularis, teres minor) and scapular stabilizers (rhomboid major and minor, trapezius, latissimus dorsi)

Soccer Focus

The bench, sometimes known as the plank, is a basic core strengthening exercise. Do not skip levels 1 and 2 to get to the hardest version. When you can do a level easily, with minimal local fatigue and discomfort, progress to the next level. The advanced versions of the bench can be quite difficult if performed without some preparatory training.

Sideways Bench

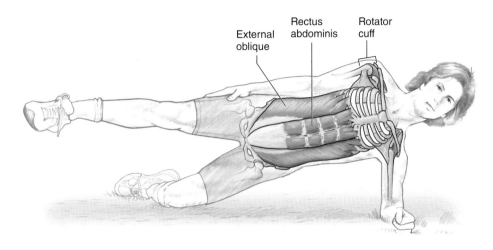

Level 1: static sideways bench.

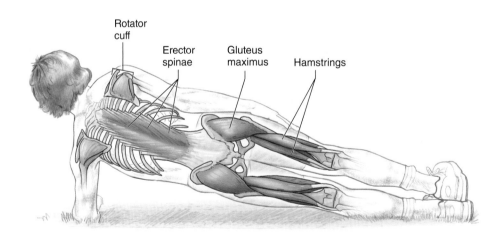

Level 2: sideways bench with hip lift.

Level 1: Static Sideways Bench

Lie on your side with the knee of your lower leg bent to 90 degrees. Rest on your forearm and knee to support your upper body. The elbow of your supporting arm should be directly under your shoulder. Lift your upper leg and hip until your shoulder, hip, and knee are in a straight line. Hold the position for 20 to 30 seconds, and then lower your body to the ground. Take a short break, switch sides, and repeat. Do this twice on both sides.

Level 2: Sideways Bench With Hip Lift

The additional movement of this variation places an extra load on the core muscles. Lie on your side with both legs straight. Lean on your forearm and the side of your lower foot so that your body is in a straight line from shoulder to foot. The elbow of your supporting arm should be directly beneath your shoulder. Lower your hip to the ground and raise it again. Repeat for 20 to 30 seconds. Take a short break, switch sides, and repeat. Do this twice on each side.

Level 3: Sideways Bench With Leg Lift

Level 3 is more challenging than level 2. Raising the leg laterally is pretty tough. Lie on your side with both legs straight. Lean on your forearm and the side of your lower foot so that your body is in a straight line from shoulder to foot. The elbow of your supporting arm should be directly beneath your shoulder. Lift your upper leg and slowly lower it again. Repeat for 20 to 30 seconds. Lower your body to the ground, take a short break, switch sides, and repeat. Do this twice for each leg.

Muscles Involved

Primary: Abdominal core, spinal extensors, gluteals, hamstrings

Secondary: Shoulder stabilizers (rotator cuff, scapular stabilizers)

Soccer Focus

The sideways bench directs the effort toward the muscles responsible for lateral control of the core. To neglect this group would neglect an important functional aspect of core control. As with the three levels of the bench exercise, do not bypass levels 1 and 2 to get to level 3. When you can do a level easily, with minimal local fatigue and discomfort, progress to the next level.

Hamstrings

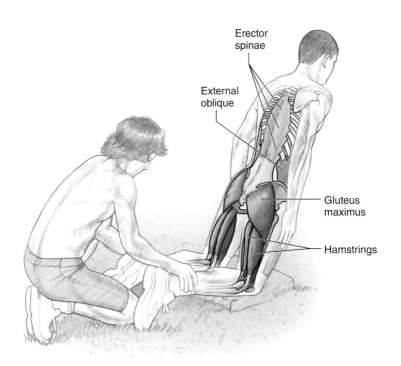

Erector spinae

External oblique

Gluteus maximus

Hamstrings

Level 1: Beginner Hamstrings

Kneel on a soft surface. Ask a partner to squat behind you and anchor your ankles to the ground. Your body should be completely straight from the shoulders to the knees throughout the exercise. You may cross your arms across your chest or simply keep your hands ready to catch your body in a push-up position. Lean forward as far as you can, controlling the movement with your hamstrings and your gluteal muscles. When you can no longer hold the position, gently absorb your weight using your hands, falling into a push-up position. Complete 3 to 5 repetitions.

Level 2: Intermediate Hamstrings

Perform the exercise as described for beginner hamstrings but complete 7 to 10 repetitions.

Level 3: Advanced Hamstrings

Perform the exercise as described for beginner hamstrings but complete 12 to 15 repetitions.

Muscles Involved

Primary: Hamstrings, gluteus maximus

Secondary: Spinal extensors, abdominal core

Soccer Focus

The pace of modern play has increased dramatically. Soccer has become a sport well suited to the high-power, ballistic sprinter. As skills and tactics evolve, so do injuries. In the 1970s, hamstring strains were rare. Today, hamstring strains are among the top four time-loss injuries in soccer. Some reports suggest a professional team can expect up to six hamstring strains or more per season. For a less severe strain, a player might be sidelined for a couple of weeks, but a more serious injury could sideline a player for four months or more. In the short, match-dense U.S. school and club-based seasons, a hamstring strain could be a season-ending injury. Thus, teams must do everything possible to prevent hamstring strains. This exercise, sometimes called the Nordic curl or Russian hamstrings, has been shown to effectively prevent hamstring strains, especially in players with a history of this injury, and should be a part of every training session. As strength improves, increase the number of repetitions you do, and try to control the descent, getting as close to the ground as possible. This exercise not only reduces the risk of hamstring strains but also strengthens the hamstrings, which helps stabilize the knee and hip when you cut or land, adding another level of protection against knee injuries.

Single-Leg Stance

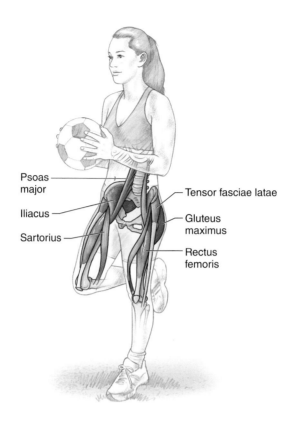

Psoas major

Iliacus

Sartorius

Tensor fasciae latae

Gluteus maximus

Rectus femoris

Level 1: single-leg stance with ball hold.

Level 1: Single-Leg Stance With Ball Hold

Holding a ball provides a small distraction, taking your mind off the act of balancing and allowing the more subconscious regions of the brain and the spinal cord to regulate balance. Balance on one leg. Hold a soccer ball with both hands. Keep your body weight on the ball of your grounded foot. Try not to let your knees buckle in. Hold for 30 seconds. Switch legs and repeat. Do this twice on each leg. You can make the exercise more difficult by moving the ball around your waist or under your raised knee.

Level 2: Single-Leg Stance With Ball Throw to Partner

Level 2 of this balance exercise adds the more demanding distraction of reacting to a ball tossed by a partner. The receiving player has to watch and track the thrown ball; predict and react to its flight; and adjust body position, balance, and posture before finally catching the ball. Stand 2 to 3 yards (2 to 3 m) away from your partner. Each of you should stand on one leg. Hold a soccer ball in both hands. While keeping your balance and holding in your abdomen, toss the ball to your partner. Keep your weight on the ball of your grounded foot. Keep your knee just slightly flexed, and try not to let it buckle in. Pay attention to controlling the supporting knee over the grounded foot to keep the knee from wobbling back and forth. Keep tossing the ball back and forth for 30 seconds. Switch legs and repeat. Do two sets for each leg.

Level 3: Single-Leg Stance With Partner Test

Level 3 of this balance exercise is even more challenging. Stand an arm's length in front of your partner as both of you balance on one foot. As you both try to keep your balance, take turns trying to push the other off balance in different directions. Try to knock your partner off balance with a gentle touch by using one or both hands to attack from different directions. You have to react quickly to the contact and respond accordingly. Try to keep your weight on the ball of your

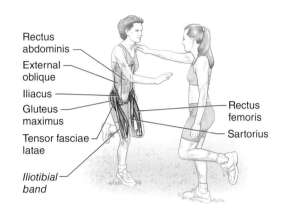

Level 3: single-leg stance with partner test.

foot and prevent your knee from buckling in. The goal is to maintain balance and keep the knee over the supporting foot. Keep this exercise under control; it's easy to get a bit out of hand. Continue for 30 seconds. Switch legs. Do two sets on each leg.

Muscles Involved

Primary: Hip flexors (psoas major and minor, iliacus, rectus femoris), hip extensors (gluteus maximus, hamstrings), tensor fasciae latae, sartorius, iliotibial band

Secondary: Abdominal core, spinal extensors

Soccer Focus

As upright beings, we are constantly maintaining our balance in an attempt to keep our center of mass over our base of support. When the center of gravity is outside a comfort radius around our base of support, we have to react and correct it or we fall. Balance is a complex physiological process that integrates environmental sensations with movement and reaction patterns by the brain and spinal cord. Special areas in the brain compare planned and actual movement information before reacting, all in milliseconds. Many knee injuries occur because of an inadequate response to a loss of balance, causing the knee to collapse in. The single-leg stance, the squat (page 34), and jumping (page 36) are directed at improving balance and knee control during a variety of activities.

Squat

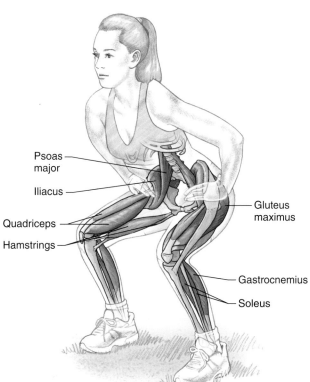

Psoas major

Iliacus

Quadriceps

Hamstrings

Gluteus maximus

Gastrocnemius

Soleus

Level 1: squat with toe raise.

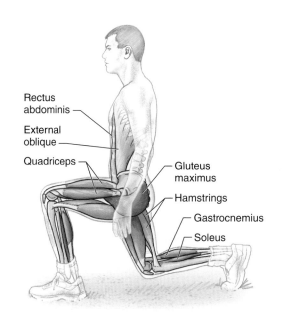

Rectus abdominis

External oblique

Quadriceps

Gluteus maximus

Hamstrings

Gastrocnemius

Soleus

Level 2: walking lunge.

Level 1: Squat With Toe Raise

This is the first of three progressively more demanding exercises designed to increase leg strength. Stand with your feet hip-width apart. Place your hands on your hips if you like. Imagine you are about to sit on a chair. Squat by bending your hips and knees to 90 degrees. Do not let your knees buckle in. Descend slowly and then straighten up more quickly. When your legs are completely straight, rise on your toes and then slowly lower back to the starting position. Continue for 30 seconds. Complete two sets.

Level 2: Walking Lunge

This level 2 exercise narrows the focus to a single leg by using the walking lunge. It may help to have a coach watch your performance from the front to ensure proper technique. The walking lunge increases dynamic flexibility of the quadriceps, hip flexors, and groin. Stand with your feet hip-width apart. Place your hands on your hips if you like. Slowly lunge forward. As you lunge, bend your leading leg until your hip and knee are flexed to 90 degrees and your trailing knee nearly touches the ground. Do not let your forward knee buckle in. Try to keep your upper body erect, with the head up and hips steady. Focus on keeping the forward knee over the foot but not beyond your toes. Do not let the knee wobble back and forth. Inhale and draw in the core during the lunge, and exhale when you stand up. Many people pause briefly between each lunge. Alternate legs as you lunge your way across the pitch (approximately 10 times on each leg), and then jog back. Do two sets across the pitch.

Level 3: One-Leg Squat

The level 3 exercise is quite challenging. It is difficult to squat on one leg and keep the knee over the grounded foot. Of all the exercises, this is probably the most difficult one for many to successfully control the knee. Have a coach watch from the front and alert you if you fail to adequately control the knee. Position yourself beside your partner, each of you standing on one leg, loosely holding onto one another for balance. Keeping the trunk as erect as possible, slowly bend your knee as far as you can but no farther than a 90-degree angle. Concentrate on preventing the knee from buckling in. Bend your knee slowly, and then straighten it a little more quickly, keeping your hips and upper body in line. Repeat the exercise 10 times and switch legs. Do two sets on each leg.

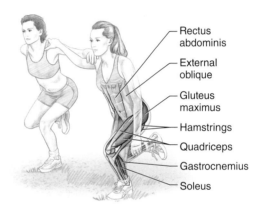

Rectus abdominis
External oblique
Gluteus maximus
Hamstrings
Quadriceps
Gastrocnemius
Soleus

Level 3: one-leg squat.

Muscles Involved

Primary: Hip flexors, gluteus maximus, quadriceps, gastrocnemius, soleus

Secondary: Abdominal core, spinal extensors, hamstrings

Soccer Focus

Another part of this prevention program is controlling how players land, either during cutting or jumping. Players who are at risk for knee injuries when landing are those who land stiffly in an erect stance. To counter this, players need to learn to land softly, absorbing the force of impact with their hips, knees, and ankles. To land softly requires you to have good ankle mobility because it is hard for the knees and hips to make up for the ankles, another example of linkage as discussed in the preface. One thought is that players who land stiffly do not have the strength to absorb the force of impact.

Jumping

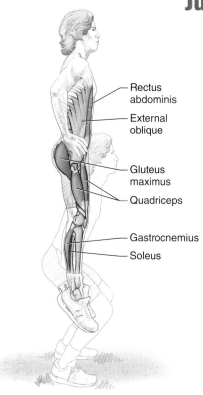

Level 1: vertical jump.

Labels on figure:
- Rectus abdominis
- External oblique
- Gluteus maximus
- Quadriceps
- Gastrocnemius
- Soleus

Level 1: Vertical Jump

Stand with your feet hip-width apart. Place your hands on your hips if you like. Imagine you are about to sit down on a chair. Bend your legs slowly until your knees are flexed to approximately 90 degrees, and hold for 2 seconds. Do not let your knees buckle in. From this squat position, jump up as high as you can. Land softly on the balls of your feet, with your hips and knees slightly bent. Repeat the exercise for 30 seconds. Rest and then perform a second set.

Level 2: Lateral Jump

Landing on one leg is more difficult, and the level 2 exercise also adds lateral movement. Landing on one leg from a lateral jump is more like a change of direction (cutting) performed in soccer. Although the exercise is markedly slower than cutting during a match, correct form, not speed, is what is important. Stand on one leg with your upper body bent slightly forward from the waist, knee and hip slightly bent. Jump approximately 1 yard (1 m) sideways from the supporting leg to the free leg. Land gently on the ball of your foot. Bend your hip and knee slightly as you land, and do not let your knee buckle in. Also control the trunk so that it remains stable. Recent research

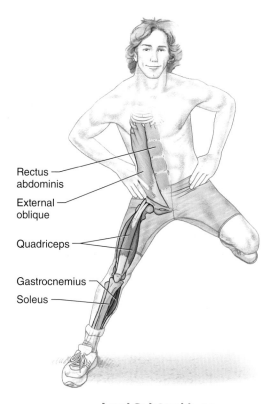

Labels on figure:
- Rectus abdominis
- External oblique
- Quadriceps
- Gastrocnemius
- Soleus

Level 2: lateral jump.

has shown that poor trunk control precedes a wobbly knee on ground contact, yet those with good trunk control also have good control of the knee.

Maintain your balance with each jump. Watch out for errors such as slight trunk rotation, lateral flexion, or both. Also watch for counterreactions from the arms in an attempt to maintain balance. If you are having trouble controlling your trunk, reduce the distance of the lateral jump until you develop adequate control. Only then should you increase the lateral distance of the jump. Repeat the exercise for 30 seconds, rest, and then perform a second set.

Level 3: Box Jump

Level 3 combines lateral, forward, and backward movement with two-foot landings. Stand with your feet hip-width apart. Imagine that a cross is marked on the ground and you are standing in the middle of it. Alternate jumping forward and backward, left and right, and diagonally across the cross. Jump as quickly and explosively as possible. Your knees and hips should be slightly bent. Land softly on the balls of your feet. Do not let your knees buckle in. Jump from point to point on the cross you have envisioned on the ground, executing the proper landing technique. Land quietly, absorbing the shock with the ankles, knees, and hips. Repeat the exercise for 30 seconds, rest, and then perform a second set.

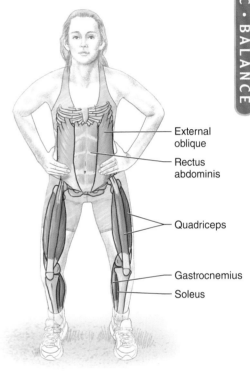

External oblique

Rectus abdominis

Quadriceps

Gastrocnemius

Soleus

Muscles Involved

Primary: Gluteus maximus, quadriceps, gastrocnemius, soleus

Secondary: Abdominal core, spinal extensors

Level 3: box jump.

Soccer Focus

Knee control when landing is a key factor in injury prevention. These three simple plyometric exercises address landing. (Plyometric exercises stretch a muscle right before it contracts.) Land softly and quietly, absorbing the force of the landing with the ankles, knees, and hips. Keep the knees over the feet, and do not let the knees collapse in.

Do not land stiff-legged when you come down from a jump. This seems to be an especially common problem in middle and high school female players. The shock of landing combined with weak hamstrings causes some players to land stiffly and erect. Landing on stiff, straight legs can cause the tibia to shift forward, putting stress on the ACL. When the knees are nearly straight, the hamstrings are at an anatomical disadvantage for resisting this forward shift of the tibia, setting up the ACL for injury. This tibial shift does not happen if you flex the knees during impact; the greater the knee flexion, the less strain on the ACL.

Running Across the Pitch

Execution

Run from one side of the pitch to the other at 75 to 80 percent of your maximum pace. Jog back and repeat a second time.

Muscles Involved

Primary: Hip flexors, quadriceps, gastrocnemius, soleus

Secondary: Hamstrings, peroneals, tibialis anterior

Soccer Focus

Chapter 1 summarizes the physical demands of soccer. About two-thirds of the game is played at a walk and a jog. Some have referred to these as *positional intensities*, when you are adjusting your position on the field in relation to ball and player movement. Faster speeds make up the other third of the game. These faster speeds—cruising and sprinting—have been termed *tactical intensities*, when you are making a concerted effort to attack or defend the goal. The warm-up is about preparing you for the upcoming training, which will include tactical training for attack or defense. Inclusion of some higher-intensity running is important to prepare your body for the harder work to come. To neglect higher-intensity running and move directly into high-intensity training would be too rapid a progression in training intensity, which increases the risk of injury.

Bounding

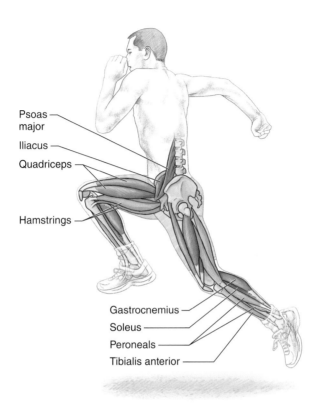

Psoas major

Iliacus

Quadriceps

Hamstrings

Gastrocnemius

Soleus

Peroneals

Tibialis anterior

Execution

Run with high bounding steps, lifting the knees high and landing gently on the balls of your feet. Exaggerate the arm swing (opposite arm and leg) for each step. Try not to let your leading leg cross the midline of your body or let your knee buckle in. Repeat the exercise until you reach the other side of the pitch, and then jog back to recover and repeat a second time.

Muscles Involved

Primary: Hip flexors, quadriceps, gastrocnemius, soleus

Secondary: Hamstrings, peroneals, tibialis anterior

Soccer Focus

Anyone who has seen a track athlete train should be familiar with this exercise. Exaggerate each step with a forceful push-off by the grounded leg and a forceful upward knee drive by the swing leg. The leg drive is aided by an exaggerated arm swing. Keep the trunk stable and erect. Do not allow the leading leg to cross the midline of the body. Keep the knee over the foot of the front leg, and do not let it go into the valgus position (see page 17) when landing.

Plant and Cut

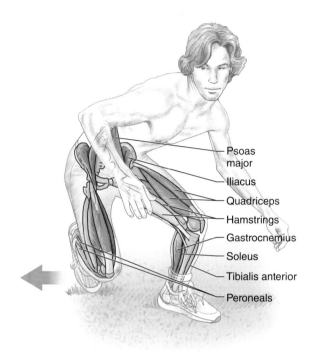

Psoas major
Iliacus
Quadriceps
Hamstrings
Gastrocnemius
Soleus
Tibialis anterior
Peroneals

Execution

Jog four or five steps, and then plant on the outside leg and cut to change direction. Accelerate and sprint five to seven steps at 80 to 90 percent of your maximum pace before you decelerate and do a new plant and cut in the opposite direction. Do not let your knee buckle in during the plant. Repeat the exercise until you reach the other side of the pitch, and then jog back and repeat a second time.

Muscles Involved

Primary: Hip flexors, quadriceps, gastrocnemius, soleus

Secondary: Hamstrings, peroneals, tibialis anterior

Soccer Focus

This exercise is about agility. Many people think agility exercises need to be done as fast as possible, but when speed is the focus, form and posture tend to falter. In this case, correct form, posture, and knee control are more important than speed. Perform this exercise quickly, but not so fast that form is sacrificed. Plant the outside foot firmly and absorb the force of impact using the ankle, knee, and hip, and then sprint off at an angle in the opposite direction.

Most fitness professionals have heard it before: Soccer is a leg game. Why should a soccer player, except perhaps the goalkeeper, pay much attention to the arms? People with these opinions should look carefully at match photos from soccer magazines or websites and note how the trunk, shoulders, and arms are used in soccer. Although the arms do not have much of a primary role in the game, the speed of play and athleticism of players today put players in such close proximity to each other that they must be able to navigate during close-quarter play. Physical contact requires adept balance, and the arms are heavily involved in maintaining balance.

Modern tactics are a combination of direct play and possession. Maintaining possession requires a player to be able to shield an opponent from the ball. Using the arms within the laws of the game helps make the player seem bigger and more difficult to displace from the ball, thereby helping him maintain possession. A system of play that is gaining popularity is the 4-5-1, in which an important trait of the single striker is the ability to maintain possession of the ball in order to play it to oncoming midfield teammates. The player who can reliably hold possession when under defensive pressure will see a lot of minutes.

If that isn't enough to convince you, look at the muscular development of some of the players on TV when they take their shirts off after a match. (If they do this in celebration after scoring, they risk getting a yellow card.) If that level of play is what you aspire to, upper-body resistance training is in your future.

Anatomy of the Upper Extremity

The upper extremity is divided into three segments. The main bone of the upper arm is the humerus, which runs from the shoulder joint to the elbow joint. The forearm runs from the elbow to the wrist. The forearm includes 2 bones, the radius and ulna. The hand and wrist make up the third segment. The wrist has 8 bones and the hand has 19 bones.

Bones, Ligaments, and Joints

The humerus is the one bone of the upper arm. The proximal end, the end toward the trunk of the body—in this case, the shoulder end of the bone—has a rounded head that articulates with the glenoid of the scapula. This is the ball portion of the ball-and-socket shoulder joint, which is discussed further in chapter 4. Around this head are areas for the attachment of muscles from the chest and upper back. As you proceed down the upper arm toward the elbow, the bone is mostly smooth, with sites for muscle attachment for the deltoid and other muscles before it widens and forms the upper portion of the elbow.

The two forearm bones are the ulna and the radius. The ulna is on the side of the little finger, and the radius is on the thumb side. A unique feature of the forearm is its ability to rotate the palm down, or pronate, and rotate the palm up, or supinate. (This is easy to remember: You would hold a bowl of soup with the palm up.) When the forearm is supinated, these two bones are parallel; when the forearm is pronated, the radius crosses over the ulna. The elbow, or proximal, end of the ulna is, for lack of a better word, a hook that wraps around the spool-shaped surface of the humerus. (When you point to your elbow, you touch the knot on the back of the joint. That knot is the ulna.) The proximal end of the radius has a flat concave disc that articulates with the rounded convex end of the humerus. Together, these two bones move around the humerus to flex (decrease the joint angle of) and extend (increase the joint angle of) the elbow. Pronation occurs when the disclike end of the radius rotates over the ulna into a palm-down position. (A similar motion occurs near the wrist.) Technically, pronation and supination occur along the forearm, not the elbow. A number of ligaments maintain the integrity of the joint and are implicated in injuries such as tennis elbow and Little League elbow. A tough ligament that lies between the radius and ulna helps keep the bones parallel and broadens the area for muscle attachment along the forearm.

The wrist and hand are very complex and are best visualized in anatomical position: palms turned forward, with the radius and ulna parallel. The wrist is made up of two parallel rows of bones (carpals), each with four small bones and small ligaments that connect both sides of adjacent bones. The proximal row of bones articulates with the distal ends of the radius and ulna, with the larger radius having the most contact. The wrist actions are flexion and extension plus the unique motions of ulnar deviation, in which the hand bends toward the ulna (decreasing the angle between the little finger and the ulna), and radial deviation, in which the hand bends toward the radius (decreasing the angle between the thumb and the radius). The distal row of carpals articulates with the five metacarpals that make up the palm of the hand. Each of these metacarpals, numbered I to V beginning on the thumb side, has a digit (finger or thumb) attached. The four fingers are made up of three phalanges (proximal, middle, and distal), while the thumb has only two (proximal and distal).

Muscles

All muscles have two attachments. The *origin* is the immobile end; the *insertion* is the movable end. In the overwhelming majority of situations, activating a muscle causes contraction that pulls the insertion toward the origin. Knowing the anatomy of the skeleton and a muscle's origin and insertion tells you the muscle's action, or how the bones move around specific joints. The muscles of the upper extremity have their primary effect on the elbow, forearm, wrist, and fingers, but in a couple of cases they also have some effect at the shoulder.

Muscles Acting on the Elbow

The elbow flexes and extends. The triceps brachii muscle (figure 3.1) of the upper arm performs extension. The word *triceps* refers to the three heads of the muscle, and *brachii* refers to the upper arm region. (Most muscle names are descriptive if you can navigate a little Latin.) The long head is the middle muscle that courses down the back of your upper arm. It originates just under the glenoid of the scapula. The medial and lateral heads originate along the long shaft of the humerus. They join together through a common tendon attaching to that knot you think of as your elbow. As the triceps pulls its insertion toward its origin, the muscle pulls on the ulna, and the result is forearm extension. The long head of the triceps also crosses the shoulder and assists in shoulder extension.

The action opposite forearm extension is forearm flexion. The biceps brachii (figure 3.2) of the upper arm performs forearm flexion. The word *biceps* refers to the two heads of the muscle. Both heads originate on the scapula. One head begins above the glenoid, opposite the long head of the triceps brachii, while the other begins on another location on the scapula underneath the deltoid. These two heads come together to form the belly of the biceps brachii, which inserts through a single tendon on the radius that is easy to see and feel.

A second forearm flexor underneath the biceps brachii is the brachialis. It begins along the anterior (front) shaft of the humerus and inserts on the anterior side of the ulna, just

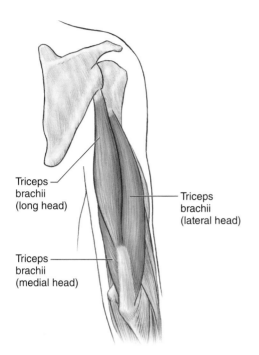

Figure 3.1 Triceps brachii muscle.

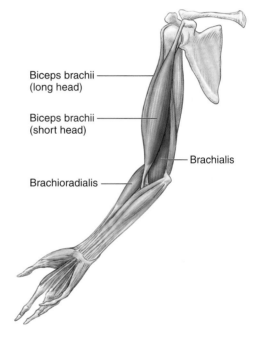

Figure 3.2 Biceps brachii, brachialis, and brachioradialis muscles.

beyond the ulna's hook. The third flexor, the brachioradialis, begins well down the shaft of the humerus and inserts on the radius down toward the base of the thumb. These three muscles work together to flex the forearm.

The biceps brachii inserts proximally on the radius. When this muscle contracts, its first order of business is to supinate the forearm. Forearm flexion is its secondary action. When the forearm is supinated, the biceps can put all its efforts into flexion. But when the forearm is pronated, the biceps tendon is sort of wrapped around the radius, so its first action is to perform supination. Pronate your right hand, and place your left hand on the biceps; feel the biceps brachii contract when you supinate your forearm.

Notice that the muscles are neatly arranged to work in opposition to each other—one group flexes and one group extends. Muscles that work in opposition to each other are said to be *antagonists*. Muscles that work together to perform the same action are called *agonists*.

Muscles Acting on the Wrist and Hand

The dexterity of the hand is a marvel of engineering. To achieve this degree of fine motor control, a large number of muscles in the forearm insert all over the wrist, hand, and fingers. The bulk of the forearm muscles (figure 3.3) originate from a common tendon coming off either the medial or lateral side of the distal humerus. These are those little bumps on either side of your elbow; you might refer to the one on the inside of your elbow as your funny bone. The tendons of the forearm pass under a tough tendinous tissue, called a retinaculum, that wraps around your wrist about where you would wear a wristband.

The muscles that perform flexion mostly originate from the medial bump and are found on the anterior side of the forearm. The extensors originate from the lateral bump and course down the posterior side of the forearm. There are a number of deeper muscles. Most forearm muscles are named for their action (flexor or extensor), location (ulnar or radial side), and insertion (carpal [wrist], digitorum [fingers], pollicis [thumb], indicis [index finger], or digiti minimi [little finger]). If you contract the muscles with *radialis* in their name, you get radial deviation. Muscles with *ulnaris* in their name perform ulnar deviation. A plethora of small intrinsic muscles in the hand assist all these muscles and also perform other actions such as spreading the fingers apart and moving the thumb.

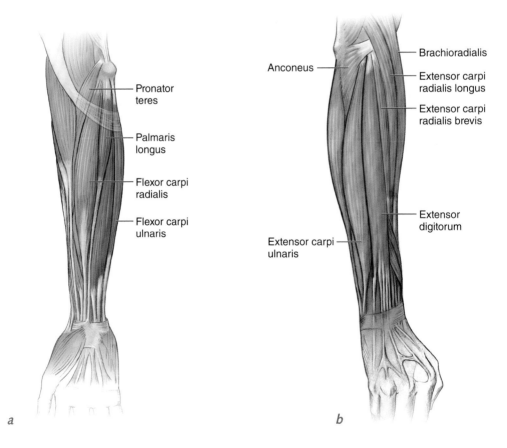

Figure 3.3   Forearm muscles: *(a)* flexors; *(b)* extensors.

The muscles that perform wrist flexion are the flexor carpi radialis, palmaris longus, and flexor carpi ulnaris. The muscles that perform wrist extension are the extensor carpi radialis longus, extensor carpi radialis brevis, and extensor carpi ulnaris. The muscles that perform finger flexion are the flexor digitorum superficialis, flexor digitorum profundus, and flexor pollicis longus. The muscles that perform finger extension are the extensor digitorum, extensor digiti minimi, extensor indicis, extensor pollicis longus, and extensor pollicis brevis.

Dip

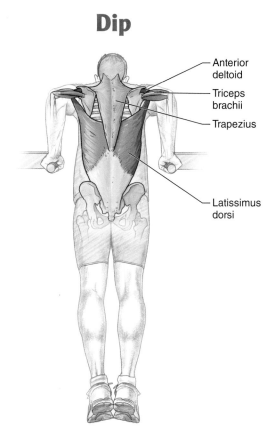

Anterior deltoid

Triceps brachii

Trapezius

Latissimus dorsi

⚠️ **SAFETY TIP** Lower your body only until your upper arms are parallel to the floor. Be sure your elbows are not above your shoulders at the lowest point of this exercise. If you do the exercise properly, you should feel a little stretch across the front of your shoulders.

Execution

1. Most weight racks include supports for doing dips. Adjust the height of the supports so that your feet do not touch the ground at the bottom of the descent.

2. Grasp the grips. Jump up and extend your elbows so your arms are straight.

3. Slowly lower your body until your upper arms are parallel to the floor. Maintain correct posture, and move the spine in a straight, vertical path.

4. Pause at the lowest level and then reverse the movement, pushing yourself back up until the elbows are fully extended. Raise the body using the arms; do not push up with the feet. Your feet are for support and balance only.

Muscles Involved

Primary: Anterior deltoid, latissimus dorsi, triceps brachii

Secondary: Pectoralis major, pectoralis minor, trapezius, brachioradialis

Soccer Focus

The dip works the triceps and shoulders. Although soccer focuses on the lower extremity, nearly every challenge from an opponent must be met with resistance using the arms and shoulders. The player who neglects the arms when training will be at a disadvantage during physical contact. Players with the ball often use an arm to keep the opponent at bay. Be cautious when using the arms during such contact. A referee may call a foul if the arm moves toward or above horizontal.

VARIATIONS

On the field, you can perform a modification of the classic dip. Use two stable benches, one for your hands and the other for your feet. Lower yourself toward the ground, moving your spine in a straight line, until your upper arms are parallel with the ground. Pause and then push back up. You can also do a dip by putting your hands on two soccer balls. The depth of the dip is reduced because the balls are not as tall as the bench. Maintaining stability on the round balls adds a dimension of reactive balance as the balls move.

Elastic Band Curl

Execution

1. This exercise can be done from a standing or seated position. Choose an elastic band with the proper level of resistance for you: light (tan, yellow), moderate (red, green), heavy (blue, black), or very heavy (silver, gold). You may have to try out several bands to determine which resistance is best for you.

2. Stand in an erect posture, with your feet about shoulder-width apart.

3. Hold an end of the elastic band in each hand, and stand on the band with both feet.

4. Perform a traditional curl motion by flexing the elbows. Return to the starting position by slowly extending the forearms. You may use both arms in unison or one arm at a time. Maintain an erect posture. Do not flex the trunk, hips, or knees during the exercise.

5. As your strength increases, perform more repetitions with the same band, shorten the band to increase the resistance, or switch to a band that supplies more resistance.

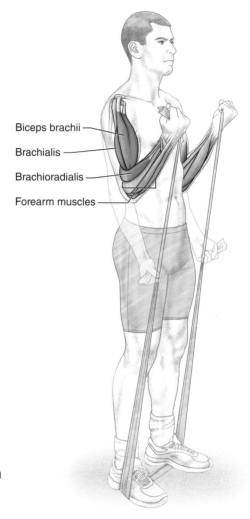

Biceps brachii

Brachialis

Brachioradialis

Forearm muscles

⚠️ **SAFETY TIP** If you arch your back, develop a swinging motion in both directions, or use your back to help with the curl, you are probably using too much resistance. Reduce the amount of resistance.

Muscles Involved

Primary: Biceps brachii, brachialis, brachioradialis

Secondary: Forearm muscles (mostly wrist and finger flexors including flexor carpi radialis and ulnaris, palmaris longus, flexor digitorum superficialis and profundus, and flexor pollicis longus) to grasp band

Soccer Focus

Improving strength during training can be a challenge. Push-ups are great for strengthening the forearm extensors and shoulders. Training the forearm flexors is more difficult but still needs to be done in order to achieve muscular balance in the upper arm. In the absence of a pull-up bar, a little creativity is needed. Elastic bands are very versatile and affordable and can be used to train most major muscle groups. Elastic bands have different degrees of resistance, usually indicated by the band's color. Using a shorter band that must be stretched from hand to hand can further increase resistance. A creative coach might use this exercise as one station in a circuit of various activities.

VARIATION

Dumbbell Curl

A dumbbell curl works the same primary muscles but allows the additional actions of pronation and supination. You can raise the dumbbell in a supinated (palm up) position and lower it in a pronated (palm down) position. When the entire curl motion is performed with the forearm in pronation (palm down), the biceps is less involved, forcing more work from the brachialis and brachioradialis. Sitting on a ball adds a balance dimension not encountered when using a stable bench.

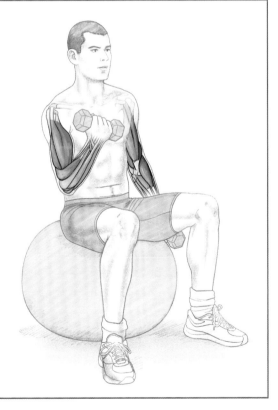

Lat Pull-Down

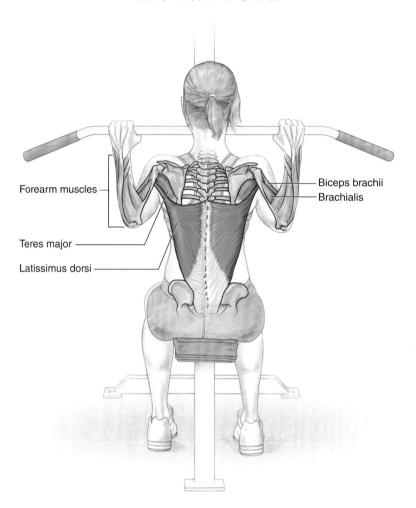

Forearm muscles

Biceps brachii

Brachialis

Teres major

Latissimus dorsi

Execution

1. Sit at a lat pull-down machine with the seat set for your body size. Adjust the seat so that the pad secures your thighs. This keeps you seated throughout the exercise.

2. Reach up and grab the ends of the bar in an overhand grip. Leading with the elbows, perform elbow flexion to start pulling the bar below the level of your chin as you squeeze your shoulder blades together. Continue to pull the bar down.

3. Slowly return the weight to the starting position.

⚠️ **SAFETY TIP** The old way to perform this exercise was to pull the bar down to touch the back of the neck, but this can increase the stress on the neck and aggravate shoulder problems. It is easy to let momentum take over when doing this exercise, so pause briefly at the end of each movement.

Muscles Involved

Primary: Latissimus dorsi, teres major

Secondary: Biceps brachii, brachialis, forearm muscles to grasp bar

Soccer Focus

Although using the outstretched arms to hold an opponent at bay is against the rules, depending on the referee, the arms and shoulders still need to be strong to resist an opponent in tight quarters. When dribbling in a crowd, you will use your arms for balance and to maintain space. The combination of the muscles of the arm and shoulder allows this. Look closely at strikers in the modern game. They have well-developed and defined arm and shoulder muscles. For

some machines that use a pulley system, you will kneel and face the device. As your strength improves and the resistance increases, you may need a partner to stand behind you and press down on your shoulders to keep you on the floor.

VARIATION

Barbell Pull-Up

Place a barbell on a weight rack high enough that you can hang from it with your feet on a weight bench. Lie under the bar and establish an overhand grip, with your hands about shoulder-width apart. Pull your body up to the bar, and then extend your arms to return to the starting position. This is sort of an upside-down push-up or bench press that also works the lats. Make sure you keep your body in a straight line when doing this. Draw in your core, too.

Seated Triceps Extension

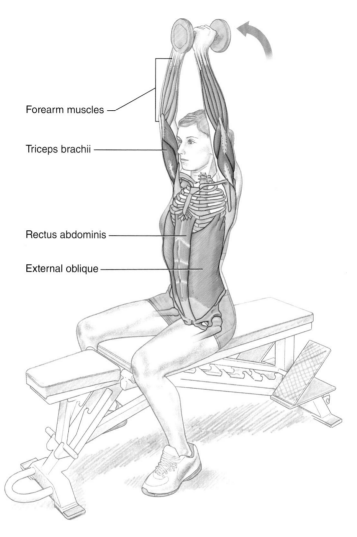

Forearm muscles

Triceps brachii

Rectus abdominis

External oblique

⚠ **SAFETY TIP** Posture is important. Keep the head aligned with the spine. Keep the elbows in a fixed position, and don't drop the shoulders to help lift the weight.

Execution

1. Sit in a chair with a low back or on a bench with no back support. Spread your legs, with your knees flexed and feet flat on the floor.
2. Hold a dumbbell vertical, wrapping both hands around the inside weight of one end of the dumbbell.
3. Raise your elbows toward the ceiling. Flex your elbows so the weight is behind your head. Keep your elbows close to your ears.
4. Extend your forearms until they are in full extension.
5. Slowly lower the weight back to the starting position. Maintain good posture with an erect back during the exercise.

Muscles Involved

Primary: Triceps brachii

Secondary: Abdominal core (external oblique, internal oblique, transversus abdominis, rectus abdominis), spinal extensors (erector spinae, multifidus), forearm muscles to grasp dumbbell

Soccer Focus

Despite the size of a large soccer field (usually 110 yards by 70 yards [100 m by 64 m]), opponents may find themselves in close quarters anywhere on the field. Although raising an arm toward vertical during a confrontation may be whistled by the ref, angling the arms toward the ground and holding them in an almost isometric contraction can make it more difficult for an opponent to make a fair attempt at obtaining

control of the ball. The focus of soccer may be on the lower extremity, but the arms play a repeated role in who obtains or maintains control of the ball.

VARIATION

Triceps Kickback

A variation is the popular triceps kickback with a dumbbell. Kneel on a weight bench, and lean forward until the trunk is about parallel with the floor. Hold the dumbbell in the arm opposite the kneeling leg so the upper arm is parallel to the trunk, and then extend the forearm to full extension. Or stand in a staggered stance with the weight in the hand opposite the leg in front. Add stability by placing the inactive hand on the forward knee.

Seated triceps extensions can be made more challenging if you sit on a large stability ball. This will require you to react to the movements of the ball as you perform the exercise. Another alternative is to perform triceps extensions with a cable machine. Face away from the cable machine, and use both hands to grab the handle over your head. Extend your elbows.

Standing Push-Down

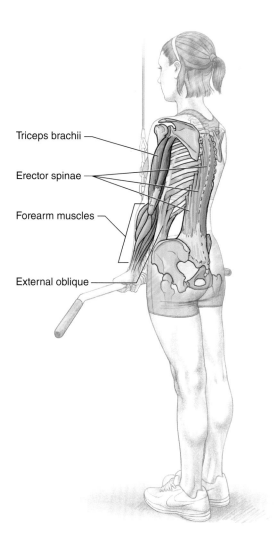

Triceps brachii

Erector spinae

Forearm muscles

External oblique

Execution

1. Stand and face a cable machine. Grasp the bar using an overhand grip, with your hands about shoulder-width apart.
2. Keep your elbows close to your body as you bring your forearms to full extension.
3. Hold the bar briefly at full extension before slowly returning the bar to the starting position.

Muscles Involved

Primary: Triceps brachii

Secondary: Abdominal core, spinal extensors, forearm muscles to grasp bar

Soccer Focus

Some sports, such as American football, favor mass, and some, such as basketball and volleyball, favor height. Soccer is a game for the masses since it does not require any particular body dimensions for those who play and enjoy the game. The typical soccer player is closer to the average height and weight for his age and gender. It is uncommon to see heavily developed players, especially in the upper body. But to neglect the upper body would mean placing oneself at a disadvantage during physical challenges.

VARIATION

Reverse Push-Down

Stand and face the cable machine. Grasp the bar in a reverse grip with the palms up. Execute the same movement. This variation works the same muscles but recruits them differently.

Barbell Curl

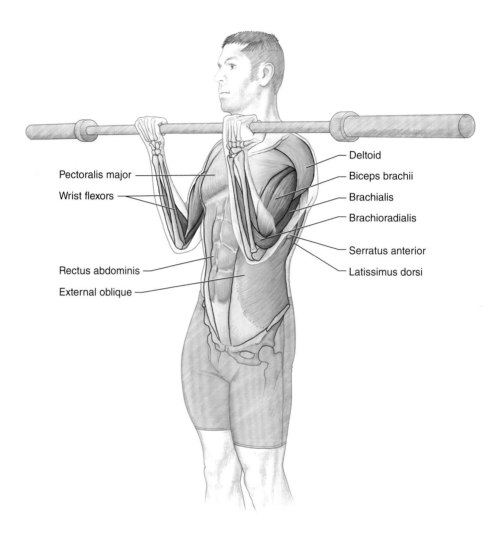

Pectoralis major

Wrist flexors

Rectus abdominis

External oblique

Deltoid

Biceps brachii

Brachialis

Brachioradialis

Serratus anterior

Latissimus dorsi

Execution

1. Stand in an erect posture, with your feet about shoulder-width apart and a barbell in front of you.
2. Grasp the bar in a supinated (palm up) grip.
3. Raise the bar by performing forearm flexion and moving the weight toward the shoulders. Lift the bar through the full range of motion. Pause briefly and then slowly lower the bar to the starting position.

⚠ **SAFETY TIP** Keep the body aligned and the spine in neutral position. Keep the movement under control—do not let momentum play a role.

Muscles Involved

Primary: Biceps brachii, brachialis, brachioradialis

Secondary: Wrist flexors (flexor carpi radialis and ulnaris, palmaris longus), stabilizers of the trunk (abdominal core, erector spinae) and shoulders (deltoid, supraspinatus, infraspinatus, subscapularis, teres minor, latissimus dorsi, pectoralis major), scapular stabilizers (serratus anterior, rhomboid major and minor, middle trapezius)

Soccer Focus

During free play on the field, the arms are used mostly to keep an opponent away from the ball or to gain a bit of an advantage when running with an opponent, within the laws of the game, of course. These actions generally do not require forearm flexion. It would be unwise, however, to focus strength training solely on actions specific to the game and neglect antagonist muscles. To do so would lead to muscle imbalances, which are not advisable for optimal muscle and joint function.

VARIATION

Machine Curl

A machine curl works the same primary muscles. Sit in a curl machine. Adjust the seat to allow access to the bar when you are in an erect posture and your feet are flat on the machine's platform. With the weight lowered, grasp the bar or handles in a supinated (palm up) grip. Raise the weight by performing forearm flexion and moving the weight toward the shoulder. Lift the weight through the full range of motion. Pause briefly and then slowly lower the weight to the starting position.

SHOULDERS AND NECK

4

In a sport such as soccer, the attention is on the lower extremities, the legs. Soccer players move and perform the bulk of their skills with the ball using the lower extremities. Often players who decide to add resistance training to their programs focus on the legs alone, but this is shortsighted. Every section of the body above the legs is recruited during play to prevent injuries, maintain balance, increase speed, generate and transfer power, maintain space, perform throw-ins, and much more.

When choosing to supplement your ball training, realize that the entire body, not just the legs, needs to be addressed. Imbalances within and between the various regions of the body can derail performance and may even increase the risk of injury. An overall fitter player will be able to delay fatigue and go deeper into a match, increasing his chances of affecting the outcome of the match. The fitter player also is more resistant to injury, and on teams that have minimal substitutes, keeping players healthy is a prime reason for supplementing training.

Anatomy of the Shoulder Joint

A joint, or articulation, is where bones come together. The three main types of joints are immovable, slightly movable, and freely movable. Examples of immovable joints are the bones of the adult skull and the joints between the three bones that make up each side of the pelvis. Examples of slightly movable joints are where the ribs connect to the sternum. Freely movable joints are what most people think of when envisioning a joint—shoulder, elbow, knee, ankle, and others—and there are different types of freely movable joints. Two of the most common injuries sustained by soccer players damage the joint integrity of the ankle or the knee.

The typical freely movable joint is encased inside a sleeve of connective tissue called the *synovial capsule*. Thickenings of this capsule at specific locations form the ligaments. Ligaments connect bone to bone, and tendons connect muscle to bone. Most ligaments are extra-articular; that is, they are outside of the joint capsule that surrounds the two bones. The notable exceptions are the anterior and posterior cruciate ligaments, which are intra-articular and are found within the joint capsule of the knee. (Learn more about the knee in chapter 8.)

The upper arm is connected to the central portion of the skeleton, which is called the axial skeleton, through what appears to be a very simple arrangement that has a complex overall function. The humerus, the upper arm bone, articulates with the glenoid, the mostly flat surface of the scapula that is made deeper by a cartilage cup called the glenoid labrum. The scapula rides on some deep muscles of the back and can slide and rotate a bit around the curved surface of the ribs. But its only connection to the axial skeleton is by way of the clavicle, or collarbone, to the sternum, or breastbone. So what we see are three distinct joints: the sternoclavicular joint (clavicle to sternum), the acromioclavicular joint (clavicle to a specific location on the scapula, the point on the top of your shoulder), and the glenohumeral joint (the flat glenoid on the scapula to the rounded head of the humerus). You may hear of a scapulothoracic joint between the scapula and the ribs, although there is no direct bony articulation between the scapula and the ribs.

The ligaments of the sternoclavicular joint are quite strong, and this joint is not injured very frequently in soccer. The acromioclavicular joint has a number of ligaments for both stability and mobility that can be injured during soccer play, mostly from a direct blow to the top of the shoulder (e.g., falling and landing on the tip of the shoulder). The glenohumeral joint is the most mobile joint in the body and is an amazing feat of biomechanical engineering. The joint capsule thickens into a number of distinct glenohumeral ligaments. This joint dislocates most often when the arm is outstretched and forced into another direction, usually backward, leading to the humerus dislocating forward or anteriorly.

> A *shoulder dislocation* occurs at the glenohumeral joint. A *shoulder separation* occurs at the acromioclavicular joint.

The body is divided into three planes. The frontal plane divides the body into front and back sections, the sagittal plane divides the body into right and left sections, and the transverse plane divides the body into upper and lower sections. All movements of the shoulder are described according to the plane in which the movement occurs. As the most mobile joint in the body, the shoulder moves in all three planes and has a number of distinct movements (see table 4.1).

Mobility is a good thing, but it also increases the potential for injury. In soccer, collisions and falls cause most of the injuries to the upper extremity and shoulder girdle. A player with strong shoulder muscles will be able to react to and withstand impact to protect the shoulder.

Table 4.1 Shoulder Movements

Plane	Movement	Description
Frontal	Flexion	Arm raised in front of body
	Extension	Arm lowered in front of body, continuing beyond trunk
Sagittal	Abduction	Arm raised out to the side
	Adduction	Arm lowered back to the side
Transverse	Internal rotation	Humerus rotated toward the midline of the body; best visualized by flexing the elbow first
	External rotation	Humerus rotated away from the midline of the body; best visualized by flexing the elbow first
	Horizontal adduction	First the arm is abducted out to the side and then moved horizontally toward the midline
	Horizontal abduction	Arm is raised in front of body and then moved horizontally away from the midline
Multiplanar	Circumduction	Arm is held parallel to the floor and swung in a wide circle (incorporates all shoulder motions)

Shoulder Muscles

Most shoulder muscles attach to the scapula. As stated in chapter 3, a muscle has two attachments. In general the *origin* is at the immobile end, while the *insertion* is at the movable end. In the majority of situations, when a muscle is stimulated and contracts, it pulls the insertion toward the origin. Most muscles cross one joint, so its action is on that one joint, but when a muscle crosses two joints, it can have an effect on both joints. When you can picture a muscle's origin and insertion, you can reason out its action.

Deltoid

The deltoid muscle group (figure 4.1) forms the cap over the shoulder joint. There are three distinct muscles: the anterior deltoid toward the front, the lateral deltoid in the middle, and the posterior deltoid toward the back. The anterior deltoid originates on the clavicle; the lateral deltoid originates on the acromion process of the scapula (that point on the top of your shoulder); and the posterior deltoid originates on the spine of the scapula, which is on the posterior surface of the scapula. These three muscles attach to a common tendon that inserts laterally (away from the midline) on the humerus.

Together, the deltoid muscle group abducts the arm. Individually, the anterior deltoid helps with shoulder flexion, and the posterior deltoid assists with shoulder extension. Put one hand over the deltoid, and perform each action. When you raise your arm as if you were answering a question (shoulder flexion), you should feel the anterior deltoid, but not the posterior deltoid, contract.

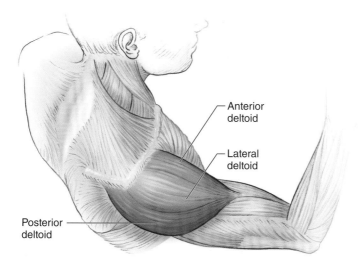

Anterior deltoid

Lateral deltoid

Posterior deltoid

Figure 4.1 Deltoid muscle group.

Rotator Cuff

The rotator cuff muscles are necessary for rotating the humerus in the glenoid, but they also are critical for shoulder stability. Unlike the hip, the shoulder does not have much in the way of structural constraints, so muscles need to provide the support. The rotator cuff (figure 4.2) is made up of four muscles. The subscapularis originates from the underside of the scapula, courses under the arm, and inserts anteriorly on the humerus. This is the main muscle for internal rotation of the humerus in the glenoid and is the muscle usually injured when a baseball pitcher tears his rotator cuff. The other three muscles of the rotator cuff are found mostly on the backside of the scapula: the supraspinatus (*supra* means it is above the spine of the scapula), infraspinatus (*infra* means it is below the spine of the scapula), and teres minor (*teres* means ropelike, and *minor* means it is the smaller of two ropelike muscles). Together, these three muscles perform external rotation of the humerus in the glenoid and assist in a number of other actions.

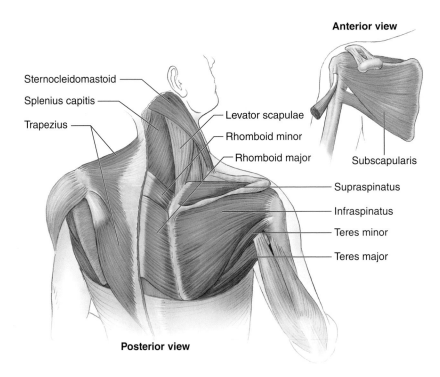

Figure 4.2   Muscles of the rotator cuff and neck.

Other Shoulder Muscles

Many other shoulder muscles help with shoulder mobility and stability:

• **Rhomboid major and minor.** These muscles originate mostly on the upper thoracic vertebrae (the vertebrae where the ribs attach) and run diagonally down, inserting on the nearby border of the scapula. The rhomboids help adduct the scapula (pull the scapula to the vertebral column), elevate the scapula (shrug the shoulders), and rotate the glenoid inferiorly (down, away from the head) because of the diagonal direction of the muscle's fibers.

• **Levator scapulae.** This muscle originates on the upper cervical vertebrae (the neck) and inserts at the upper corner of the scapula. By its name, it elevates the scapula, but it also assists in rotating the glenoid inferiorly as well as in scapular adduction.

• **Serratus anterior.** This muscle can be difficult to visualize. It originates on the lateral surface (away from the midline) of a number of ribs and follows the ribs back toward the vertical border where the rhomboids insert. When activated, the serratus anterior pulls the scapula around the surface of the ribs, away from the vertebral column. Picture the movement of the scapula when someone performs a boxing jab. This muscle is addressed again in chapter 5.

• **Trapezius.** This broad, flat muscle of the upper back is just under the skin. It originates all along the cervical and thoracic vertebral column and inserts at the lateral end of the spine of the scapula to adduct the scapula. Functionally, the trapezius is three muscles: upper, middle, and lower. The upper trapezius elevates and rotates the glenoid down, while the lower trapezius rotates the glenoid up and stabilizes the scapula to prevent rotation.

Neck Muscles

The neck is very mobile, but it is also a fragile area of the body. Because of heading, the neck muscles figure prominently in soccer. The motions of the neck include flexion (moving the chin down) and extension (moving the chin up), lateral flexion (tilting the head toward either shoulder), and rotation (turning the head). These actions can be combined for circular motions.

The primary neck flexor is the sternocleidomastoid, which originates on the clavicle and sternum, inserting on the mastoid of the skull (that knot behind your ear). The sternocleidomastoid also turns the head right or left; contracting the muscle on the right side turns the face to the left and vice versa. The main neck extensor is the splenius capitis, which originates on a number of vertebrae and inserts at the base of the skull. The levator scapulae and upper trapezius assist in neck extension. Lateral flexion is accomplished by contracting these muscles on the right or left side to move the head in the appropriate direction.

Seal Crawl

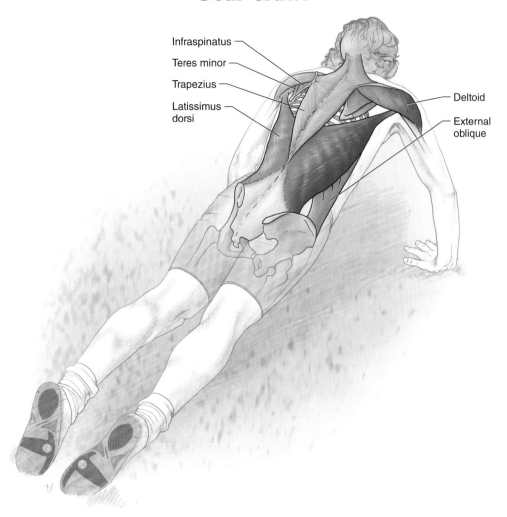

Infraspinatus
Teres minor
Trapezius
Latissimus dorsi
Deltoid
External oblique

Execution

1. Lie on the ground. Get into the up position of a traditional push-up but on your insteps, not your toes. Keep your insteps on the ground for this exercise.

2. Using only your arms for propulsion, crawl around, dragging your legs. Changing directions and speed involves more muscles, so do not crawl in a straight line. Keep your back and hips straight, and do not allow your trunk to sag toward the ground. Go farther and faster as your strength improves.

Muscles Involved

Primary: Latissimus dorsi, deltoid

Secondary: Rotator cuff (subscapularis, supraspinatus, infraspinatus, teres minor), trapezius, spinal extensors (erector spinae, multifidus) and abdominal core (external oblique, internal oblique, transversus abdominis, rectus abdominis) to maintain a straight back

Soccer Focus

The shoulder joint is very complex. Unlike the hip, the shoulder has little structural bone support. The lack of bony restraint allows for extensive motion around the shoulder. About 15 muscles attach to the scapula, clavicle, and humerus to manage this movement. Exercising each muscle and movement separately would require a lot of time and special equipment. Choose exercises that work multiple muscles in many different movements to make the most of your training time. The seal crawl requires functional motion and support from most of the shoulder, back, and abdominal muscles. This is a good general exercise for every player but especially for young players who tend to have weak shoulders.

VARIATION

Wheelbarrow

The wheelbarrow exercise requires a partner. While performing the action, you provide the pace of movement, not your partner. You pull; your partner does not push. Keep your back straight. If you have trouble keeping your back straight, have your partner hold your legs farther up toward your thighs.

⚠ **SAFETY TIP** Even if your back sags a bit when you perform the seal crawl, try to keep it straight when performing the wheelbarrow. It is best to perform these exercises on a safe surface such as grass or the floor. Avoid surfaces littered with debris that might cut or injure the hands.

Arm Wrestling

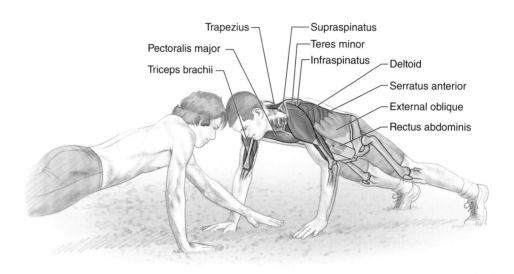

Execution

1. You will need a partner for this exercise. You and your partner lie facedown on the ground with your heads nearly touching. Get in the up position for a traditional push-up.

2. On your coach's command, try to touch or gently slap your partner's hands while trying to avoid being touched or slapped by your partner. Although some movement may occur, try to stay in the same place.

3. The duration of this exercise will vary according to arm and abdominal strength. First perform the exercise for 15 seconds, and increase the time as fitness improves.

Muscles Involved

Primary: Triceps brachii, pectoralis major, deltoid, serratus anterior, trapezius

Secondary: Rotator cuff, spinal extensors, abdominal core

Soccer Focus

This is a good exercise for working a wide range of muscles—the abdominals and back muscles for posture, the muscles that attach to the humerus to maintain the desired position and balance when one hand is off the ground, and the muscles that attach to the scapula to control the shoulders as you challenge each other. This exercise improves strength, balance, and local muscle endurance of the shoulders, arms, trunk, and back. Improvements in these aspects of muscle function will help you play deeper into the match and resist fatigue. Training is not just about the legs and the heart. Training for a whole-body activity such as soccer means addressing the whole body. Focusing only on the legs is a common error when training.

VARIATION

Grasp right hands with your partner while balancing on your left arms (or left hands, if you both are left handed). Your goal is to put your partner off balance while maintaining your own balance. Begin by simply grasping hands and holding this position. Once you both can maintain balance, add the combative element. It may take some practice to advance to using the nondominant arm, but that is a goal. Don't focus only on the dominant arm.

Head–Ball–Head Isometrics

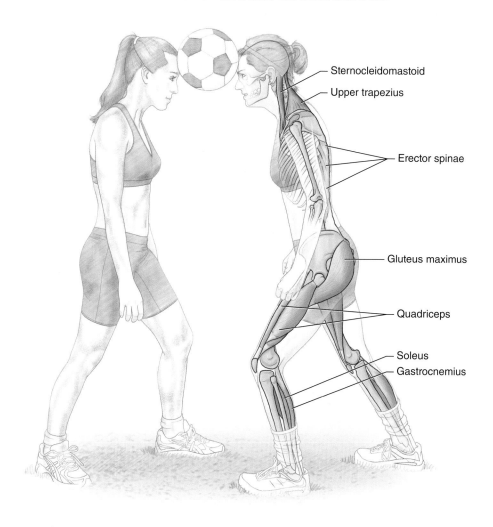

Sternocleidomastoid

Upper trapezius

Erector spinae

Gluteus maximus

Quadriceps

Soleus

Gastrocnemius

⚠️ **SAFETY TIP** Trying to best your partner could make the ball pop out and cause you to bump heads. Be careful. This isn't about winning.

Execution

1. Find a partner of similar height and weight. Stand in a staggered stance facing each other. Pin the ball between your foreheads. You may find it helpful to hold each other's upper arms.

2. Push with your legs through the trunk, neck, and ball in an attempt to push your partner back as your partner attempts to push you back. Keep the ball pinned between your heads. *This is not a competitive exercise*. You are not trying to beat your partner. The idea is to squeeze the ball.

3. At first perform a few repetitions of 10 seconds each. As you get stronger, increase the number and duration of repetitions.

Muscles Involved

Primary: Sternocleidomastoid, upper trapezius

Secondary: Gastrocnemius, soleus, quadriceps (vastus medialis, vastus lateralis, vastus intermedius, rectus femoris), gluteus maximus, spinal extensors

Soccer Focus

For very young players, heading the ball is more of a novelty that usually happens from a bounced or thrown ball. Most very young players are unable to consistently get the ball airborne or master the movements necessary to properly head the ball, making heading a pretty rare skill. As players age and grow, heading takes on an integral role in the game, making it necessary to devise ways to increase neck strength. Neck strength is important not only for heading but also to protect the head during collisions. The head is protected when the neck muscles contract to anchor the head to the much heavier torso. When the neck muscles are not strong enough, the head can jerk, causing whiplash or concussion even in the absence of a direct blow to the head.

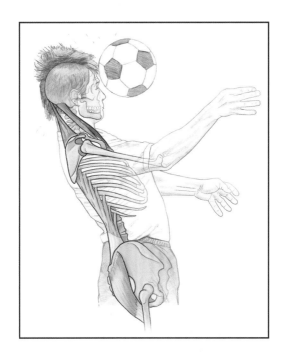

Partner-Assisted Neck Resistance

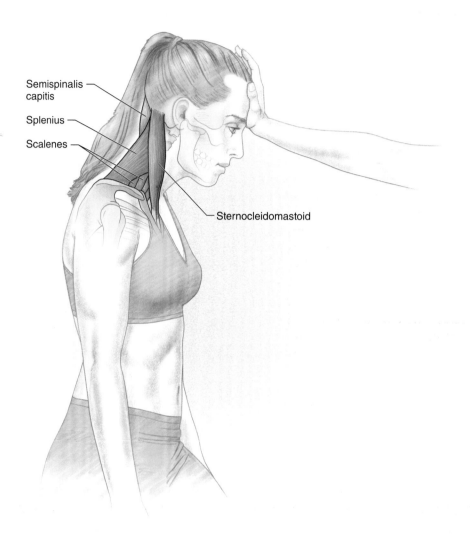

Semispinalis capitis

Splenius

Scalenes

Sternocleidomastoid

Execution

1. Find a partner of similar height and weight. Your partner will provide resistance to you as you perform the exercise. Have your partner stand in front of you with her arm extended and the palm of her hand on your forehead.

2. Flex your neck forward against the resistance provided by your partner. Your partner should provide resistance but still allow you to move through the full range of motion. The strength of this movement comes from the neck, not the trunk.

3. Repeat the exercise for all directions of movement. This can be repeated for neck extension (partner's hand on the back of your head) as well as to both sides for lateral flexion (partner's hand on one side of the head and then the other).

Muscles Involved

Primary: Sternocleidomastoid (forward flexion, lateral flexion), splenius (extension), upper trapezius (backward extension, lateral flexion)

Secondary: Neck stabilizers (such as splenius, semispinalis capitis, and scalenes)

Soccer Focus

Heading is a complex skill that does not come naturally. Why would anyone voluntarily put his head in the path of a fast-moving object? Most teams have players who will do anything to get their heads on the ball and players who will go out of their way to avoid heading the ball. Consider the difficulty of heading. When the ball is in the air, the player must decide where on the field he needs to be to head the ball and what speed and direction are necessary to get there. When he heads the ball, will he be standing or running and, if running, in what direction? Will he have to jump? How high? Off one leg or two? Where will he redirect the ball? In the air, to the ground, to a teammate? If to a teammate, should he direct the ball to his teammate's feet, in the path he is running, or somewhere else? If the header is a shot on goal, the goalkeeper must be avoided, so where is the goalkeeper? Few of these decisions involve an opponent, and all decisions must be made well ahead of impact with the ball or the opponent. It's a wonder anyone really wants to head a ball. But when done well, heading is an electrifying skill that can thrill player and spectator alike.

VARIATIONS

There are a number of variations to this exercise. One involves a towel. Your partner stands in front of you and drapes a towel around the back of your head, holding both ends. You perform neck extension against the resistance of the towel. Your partner stands opposite the movement you perform instead of in the direction of your movement as in the main exercise. If you don't have a partner, another variation is to perform isometrics by squeezing the ball against a wall using the various neck motions.

Floor Bridge

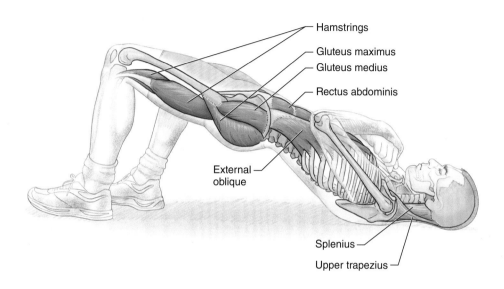

Hamstrings

Gluteus maximus

Gluteus medius

Rectus abdominis

External oblique

Splenius

Upper trapezius

⚠ SAFETY TIP At the top of the bridge, the shoulders should be in contact with the floor. This should not put any strain on the head or neck.

Execution

1. Lie on your back with your knees bent, feet flat on the floor and spread about hip-width apart. You may need to spread your arms to your sides for balance.

2. Raise your hips and trunk until your body forms a straight line from your knees to your shoulders.

3. Pause at the top position for a couple of seconds, and draw in your core. Slowly lower your trunk nearly to the ground. Hold this position and repeat. Start with five repetitions, and progress as strength improves.

Muscles Involved

Primary: Hamstrings (biceps femoris, semitendinosus, semimembranosus), gluteus maximus, gluteus medius, abdominal core

Secondary: Upper trapezius, splenius, spinal extensors

Soccer Focus

In years past, supplemental training for the neck was limited to neck bridges borrowed from wrestling. In wrestling, neck bridging is an important skill to keep from being pinned, but it is largely isometric and mostly involves neck extension and hyperextension. In soccer, a strong neck not only helps with heading but also is important for stabilizing the head during collisions with the ball, other players, the ground, the goalposts, and more. But there are other options for improving support from the neck and shoulders. Although this is most commonly thought of as a core exercise, the neck and shoulders are one of three points of ground contact and have to work against the push applied by the feet. They are also activated when the trunk is elevated. Be sure to keep the glutes contracted and the abdominals drawn in throughout the exercise.

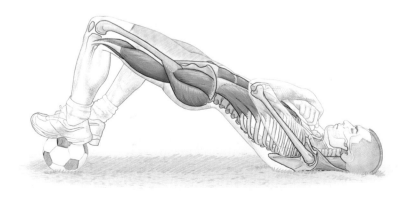

VARIATION

An element of balance can be added very easily. Instead of placing your feet on the ground for this bridge exercise, place your feet on a ball. Adding an unstable element and a narrower base of support greatly increases the difficulty of the exercise. In the gym, you can do this exercise with your feet on a large stability ball.

Pull-Up

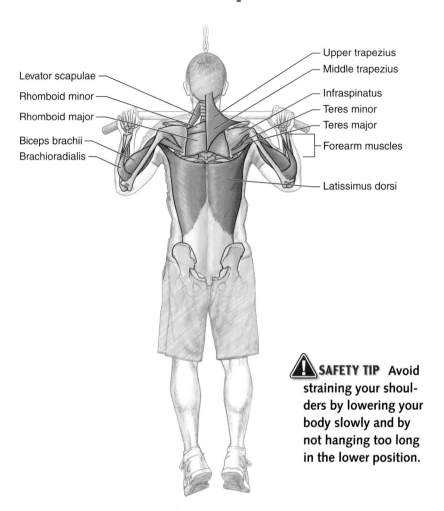

Levator scapulae

Rhomboid minor

Rhomboid major

Biceps brachii

Brachioradialis

Upper trapezius

Middle trapezius

Infraspinatus

Teres minor

Teres major

Forearm muscles

Latissimus dorsi

⚠ **SAFETY TIP** Avoid straining your shoulders by lowering your body slowly and by not hanging too long in the lower position.

Execution

1. With your hands a bit more than shoulder-width apart, grasp an overhead horizontal bar or handles on a pull-up rack, palms turned away from you.
2. Inhale and draw the navel in. Pull the body weight up until the chin is over the bar. Exhale at the point of greatest difficulty.
3. Slowly return to the starting position and repeat. Do as many as you can.

Muscles Involved

Primary: Latissimus dorsi, upper and middle trapezius, biceps brachii, brachioradialis

Secondary: Levator scapulae, rhomboid major and minor, teres major and minor, infraspinatus, forearm muscles (mostly wrist and finger flexors including flexor carpi radialis and ulnaris, palmaris longus, flexor digitorum superficialis and profundus, and flexor pollicis longus) to grasp bar

Soccer Focus

Many of the exercises in this book use body mass as the resistance. The classic pull-up is a multijoint exercise that uses body mass as resistance and is still hard to beat. For general, all-around work on the shoulders, you could do push-ups, pull-ups, and dips and expect to work almost every muscle with an attachment to the scapula and humerus. Although the pull-up increases strength, it also improves local muscle endurance because improvements are generally seen as increased repetitions. For greater strength, some athletes add resistance and intensity by hanging a free weight to a belt and wearing it around the waist.

VARIATION

Palms up or palms down? Most agree that a pull-up with the palms up is somewhat easier than a pull-up with the palms down. The reason is anatomy. The biceps brachii originates on the scapula and inserts on the radius. The brachialis originates on the humerus and inserts on the ulna. The motion of the ulna is elbow flexion and extension like the radius, but the radius also rotates over the ulna for forearm pronation and supination. The biceps is a supinator first and an elbow flexor second, while the brachialis is only a forearm flexor. When pull-ups are done with the palms up, the biceps doesn't need to supinate, so these two muscles work together to flex the elbow. When the palms are down, the biceps tries to supinate, leaving the brachialis to act without much help, making the exercise harder.

One-Arm Dumbbell Row

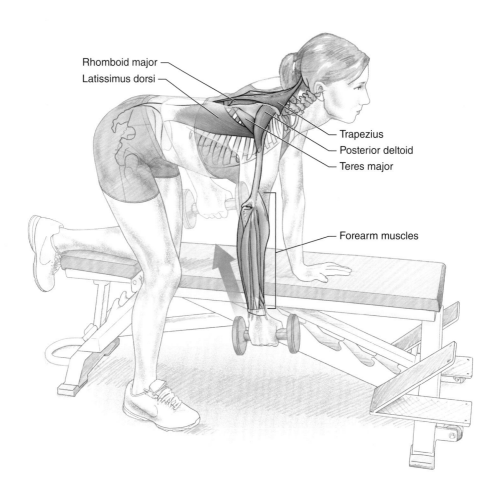

Rhomboid major

Latissimus dorsi

Trapezius

Posterior deltoid

Teres major

Forearm muscles

Execution

1. Kneel on your left knee on a padded bench. Add support by placing your left hand on the bench. Your right foot is flat on the floor, as is a dumbbell.

2. Lean forward at the hip while keeping the spine straight, and grasp the dumbbell.

3. Inhale as you raise the arm and flex the elbow as high as possible, lifting the weight to the trunk.

4. Pause at the top of the lift, and then exhale as you lower the weight until the arm is fully extended. The motion is similar to sawing wood.

Muscles Involved

Primary: Latissimus dorsi, teres major, posterior deltoid, trapezius, rhomboid major and minor

Secondary: Forearm muscles, spinal extensors for posture

Soccer Focus

Modern soccer tactics are twofold. On offense, the team tries to make the field as big as possible to give players room to maneuver and spread the defense thin. On defense, the team tries to make the field as small as possible so the team defense is very compact, and each defender is close to the ball. Players inevitably find themselves in very close quarters while competing for the ball. One of the best ways players, especially strikers, can keep a defender away from the ball is to shield the defender from the ball. This requires back and shoulder strength to make the attacking player seem bigger than he really is and avoid the wrath of the referee for unfair use of the arms. A player who is adept at screening defenders and able to maintain possession of the ball will play a lot of minutes. Possession is a big part of the game, so being able to screen defenders away from the ball is a critical and often overlooked skill.

VARIATIONS

Posture is important during rowing exercises. The standing row is a complex exercise, like many barbell lifts. You must raise the weighted bar off the floor to the thighs and then assume the specific posture before executing the row. T-bar rows, especially when performed while lying on a bench, provide support for the trunk and offer a measure of safety. Many cable machines are capable of a rowing motion that isolates the movement for safe execution of the lift.

Prone Dumbbell Fly

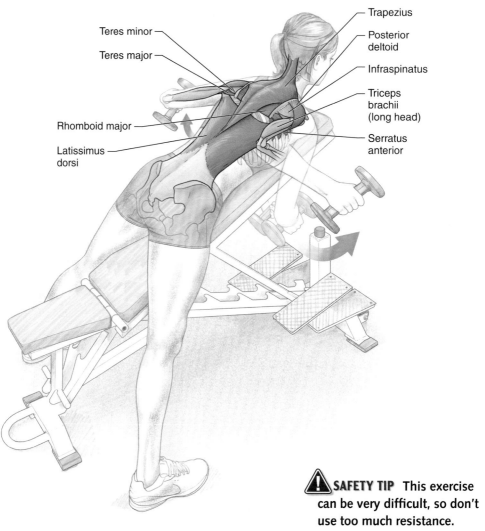

Teres minor

Teres major

Rhomboid major

Latissimus dorsi

Trapezius

Posterior deltoid

Infraspinatus

Triceps brachii (long head)

Serratus anterior

⚠ **SAFETY TIP** This exercise can be very difficult, so don't use too much resistance.

Execution

1. Lie prone on a padded bench. Your head or neck may hang over the end of the bench. Be sure the bench is well grounded and not at all unstable. Two dumbbells are on the floor on either side of the bench.

2. Grasp the weights. With elbows slightly flexed, inhale and raise your arms to lift the weights, attempting to make the arms horizontal to the floor.

3. Slowly lower the weights as you exhale.

Muscles Involved

Primary: Trapezius, rhomboid major and minor, serratus anterior, posterior deltoid, teres major, latissimus dorsi

Secondary: Triceps brachii (long head), erector spinae, rotator cuff

Soccer Focus

Watch what goes on in the penalty area of a professional match as players prepare to receive a corner kick. The pushing, shoving, grabbing, holding off, and fighting for position in the seconds just before the actual kick might surprise you. A corner kick is a scoring opportunity that has a good enough probability for success that players will be very aggressive when establishing their positions to either deflect or defend the approaching ball. (Interestingly, the scoring probability for a corner kick is not as high as you might expect. Only about 2 percent of corner kicks result in goals. One coach told me his team went 1 for more than 100 in one season.) A striker who is being counted on to gain an advantageous position for these opportunities will not be very effective if he isn't able to use his arms within the laws of the game to maintain his position in the crowded penalty area.

VARIATION

Bent-Over Row

A bent-over row is a good alternative to the prone dumbbell fly. Maintain good spinal posture when performing the bent-over row; don't round the back. This exercise mainly works the muscles that attach to the scapula—the muscles that help maintain good scapular motion, shoulder flexibility, and range of motion.

Neck Machine Flexion and Extension

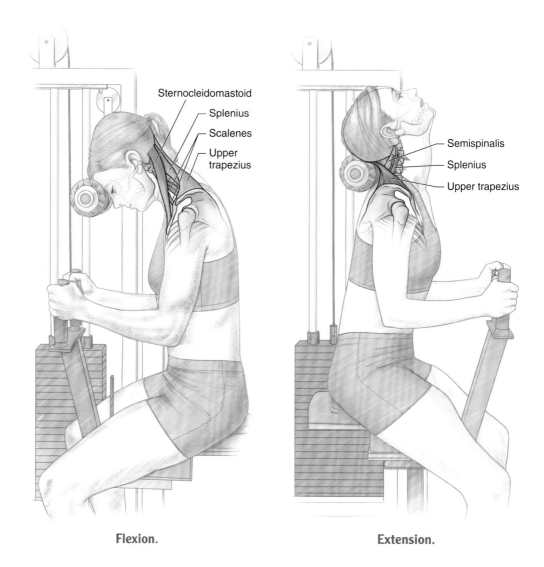

Sternocleidomastoid
Splenius
Scalenes
Upper trapezius

Semispinalis
Splenius
Upper trapezius

Flexion. Extension.

Execution

1. Adjust the seat position for your height. Sit erect with your feet flat on the floor and grasp the handles (if your machine has handles). Begin with the neck in a bit of an extended position.

2. For flexion, place your forehead on the pad. (The pad on some machines accommodates the entire face.) Flex your neck by drawing the chin down toward the chest. Pause and then return to the starting position.

3. For extension, turn around on the seat, and place the back of your head on the pad. This time, begin with the neck in a bit of a flexed position. Perform neck extension by raising your chin toward the ceiling. Pause and then return to the starting position.

Muscles Involved

Primary: Sternocleidomastoid (flexion), upper trapezius (extension), splenius (extension)

Secondary: Scalenes (flexion), splenius (flexion), upper trapezius (flexion), semispinalis (extension)

Soccer Focus

Good neck strength is important for the skill of heading as well as for protecting the head during inevitable collisions. Despite this, surprisingly few coaches include neck strengthening in their training programs. Much of the power for heading comes from the trunk, while part of the finer touch comes from the neck's action on the head to send the ball in the desired direction. Mostly flexion is used, but rotation, which is a more complex skill, is also possible. And one cannot discount the role of a strong neck in stabilizing the head so that head acceleration during collisions is minimized.

Dumbbell Shoulder Press

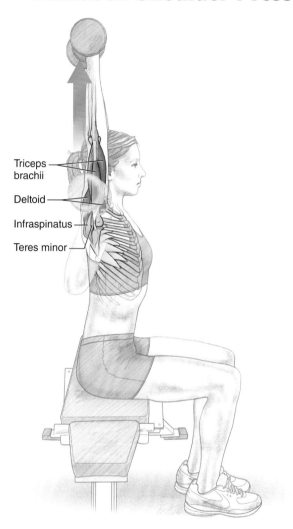

Triceps brachii

Deltoid

Infraspinatus

Teres minor

⚠️ **SAFETY TIP** Begin with a low weight. You need some initial strength to be able to control the weight when it is overhead.

Execution

1. Sit on a weight bench with your back straight and your feet flat on the floor.
2. Hold a dumbbell in each hand using an overhand grip. Hold the weights at shoulder level.
3. Extend one arm vertically. Briefly hold at the top, and then slowly lower the weight to the shoulder. Exhale when raising the weight, and inhale when lowering the weight.
4. Repeat with the other arm, and do an equal number of repetitions for each arm.

Muscles Involved

Primary: Triceps brachii, deltoid

Secondary: Shoulder stabilizers (rhomboid major and minor, trapezius, levator scapulae, rotator cuff)

Soccer Focus

It is pretty hard to envision this movement as a primary action during soccer. A team picture might suggest that the goalkeeper likely has the most developed shoulders because the arms are integral to his game. That should not mean players other than goalkeepers should neglect this and similar exercises. A well-rounded supplemental strength training program will address all motions, including the shoulders, despite the minor role some motions might appear to play in any particular sport. Because of the speed of play and the amount of contact in the game, all players must be prepared for contact. As described, the dumbbell shoulder press is a unilateral exercise (one side at a time), but it can be made a bilateral exercise if you extend both arms in unison.

VARIATION

Machine Shoulder Press

As with all free weight exercises, the dumbbell shoulder press requires a certain degree of skill to perform correctly. One of the benefits of commercial machines is that you are fixed into a specific motion and the weights are supported. This provides a measure of safety for the exercise.

Soccer players might be hesitant to enter a strength training program for any number of reasons—lack of understanding, tradition, concern that bulking up might have a negative impact on play, and so on. One reason might be simply not having access to the equipment. Part of the purpose of this book is to show exercises that can be done either on the field or in the weight room. A player who does attempt some strength training might focus only on the legs, which could lead to imbalances throughout the body, increasing the risk of injury. Players and coaches must realize that a strength training program is for the entire body, not just the legs. All regions of the body, including the chest, must be addressed.

Many athletes think of the bench press when they think about developing the chest. Although the pectoralis major is the largest and most obvious chest muscle, others also play a role in how the shoulder girdle and upper extremities operate.

Bones, Ligaments, and Joints of the Chest

In the torso, there are 10 pairs of ribs that attach in the back to the vertebral column and in the front to the sternum, with 2 pairs of ribs that attach in the back but not to the sternum. Ribs 1, 11, and 12 have a 1:1 attachment with their corresponding vertebrae, while ribs 2 through 10 attach between two vertebrae. The bone of each rib ends at roughly nipple level and is then connected to the sternum by the costal cartilage (the Latin *costa* means *rib*) to form a cartilaginous joint that has only slight mobility. Ribs 1 through 7 are called *true ribs* because each attaches directly to the sternum through the costal cartilage. Ribs 8 through 10 are called *false ribs* because their cartilage attaches to the cartilage of the rib above before eventually attaching to the sternum. The small ribs 11 and 12 are called *floating ribs* because they have no sternal attachment. Between each pair of ribs is a pair of small muscles called the intercostals that aid in breathing. The floor of the rib cage is made up of the diaphragm. Movements of the ribs play a role in inhalation and exhalation, and their cagelike arrangement protects the heart, lungs, large blood vessels, nerves, and passages that conduct air to and from the lungs. The most common chest injury is a rib fracture from some form of ballistic impact, usually to the middle ribs.

The sternum, or breastbone, is made up of three bones that fuse during growth. If you slide a finger down your sternum you will feel a horizontal ridge one-quarter to one-third of the way down the bone. This is one of the fusion points. The third bone is a fragile extension called the xiphoid process off the bottom end of the sternum. It comes off the underside of the sternum, and the amount of covering tissue makes it difficult to feel.

The sternum is important because it is the only point of bony attachment connecting the central (axial) skeleton and the upper extremities. This sternoclavicular joint is quite strong because of the ligaments and cartilage from the clavicle to the sternum, a ligament connecting the two clavicles, and ligaments that connect the clavicle to the first rib. These all work together to maintain the integrity of this joint. Despite all these stabilizing tissues, there is some movement, so it has many of the features of the typical freely movable joint. This joint is rarely injured. Usually the clavicle fractures before this joint dislocates. But injuries can happen. Think of the rodeo rider who falls from a height, cartwheels in the air, and lands on an outstretched arm.

The scapula attaches to the clavicle. Although the scapula glides over the curvature of the ribs, there are no bony articulations between the scapula and the ribs. Muscles that originate from the sternum and ribs, however, can also have their insertion on the scapula and exercise some control over the scapula's movements.

Chest Muscles

For most everyone, chest muscles and the pectoralis major muscle are synonymous (the Latin *pectus* means *chest*). The pectoralis major muscle (figure 5.1) is the largest but not the only muscle of the chest. Because of its broad origination from the sternum and costal cartilages of ribs 2 through 6 (sternal head, or lower pectoralis) as well as the clavicle (clavicular head, or upper pectoralis), it is sometimes referred to as having two distinct origins. The muscle angles toward the shoulder, inserting on the chest side of the upper humerus. Remember that a muscle pulls the insertion toward the origin. Because it inserts on a highly mobile bone, the pectoralis major has a number of primary and secondary actions on the humerus. Primary functions include horizontal adduction (arm parallel to the ground and out to the side moves across the chest), shoulder adduction, internal rotation of the humerus, and shoulder extension. You can feel the pectoralis major contract by placing a hand on the muscle and doing any of those actions. Through the connection of the humerus with the glenoid of the scapula, the pectoralis major also assists in some movements of the scapula.

Completely covered by the pectoralis major is the smaller pectoralis minor. (In anatomy, if there is a *major* there probably is a *minor*.) The pectoralis minor originates on the outer surface of ribs 3 through 5 and, with the short head of the biceps, attaches on the scapula to abduct the scapula (move the scapula along the curve of the ribs, away from the midline), depress the scapula, and help rotate the glenoid down.

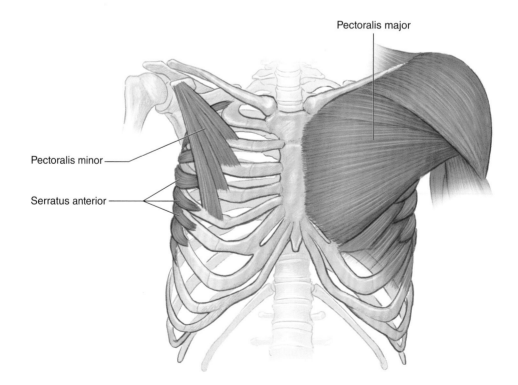

Figure 5.1   Muscles of the chest.

The final major muscle of the chest is the serratus anterior, so called because of its serrated appearance. (Think of the serrated edge of a steak knife.) The serratus anterior originates laterally on the surface of the upper 8 or 9 ribs and courses posteriorly, following the curve of the ribs to insert on the lower half of the border of the scapula that is adjacent to the vertebral column. The muscle's primary action is to abduct the scapula (move it away from the vertebral column), but it also assists in upward rotation of the glenoid (raising your arm as if in response to a question). The serratus anterior could be considered either a chest muscle because of its origin on the ribs or a scapular muscle because of its insertion on the scapula.

Think of all the muscles of the upper back and shoulder that are fully balanced by just these three muscles. That means nearly any exercise that addresses the humerus and scapula will require these muscles, while the opposing (antagonistic) muscles can nearly be singled out by specific exercises. Although most of the motions of the arms and shoulders in soccer are meant to widen your presence and make it harder for the opponent to get to the ball, it is wise to train the opposing chest muscles to maintain neuromuscular balance.

Soccer Ball Push-Up

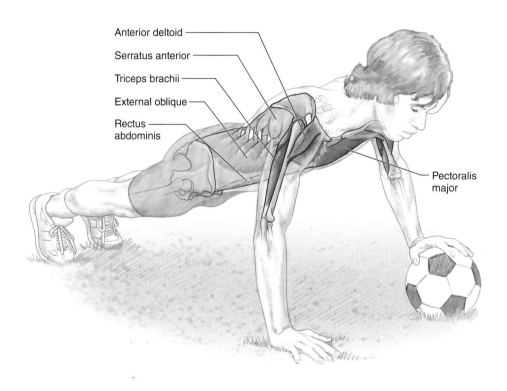

Anterior deltoid

Serratus anterior

Triceps brachii

External oblique

Rectus abdominis

Pectoralis major

Execution

1. Lie on the ground. Get into the up position of a traditional push-up, with your hands a bit wider than shoulder-width apart. Stay up on your toes with your feet together.
2. Carefully transfer one hand to the top of a soccer ball.
3. Perform a routine push-up.
4. After doing a few push-ups with one hand on the ball, stop, switch hands, and continue. Perform push-ups with the ball under the other hand.

Muscles Involved

Primary: Pectoralis major, triceps brachii, anterior deltoid

Secondary: Serratus anterior, abdominal core (external oblique, internal oblique, transversus abdominis, rectus abdominis) and spinal extensors (erector spinae, multifidus) for proper posture

Soccer Focus

The modern game is far more physical than the game played by earlier generations. The speed and athleticism of the modern player means a defender can close down a striker in the wink of an eye, and this means contact. The amount of pushing and shoving that goes on in a crowded penalty area during a corner kick would probably surprise most nonplayers. It should be intuitive that the stronger player will be better suited to handle the contact of the game. Although much of the strength necessary is initiated from the legs, the chain of actions continues up the trunk to the rest of the body. In this exercise, the height added by the ball means the body can be lowered farther than when both hands are on the ground. In addition, some reactive balance is needed because the ball can move.

VARIATION

Soccer Ball Push-Up With Two Balls

You can improve your skill with push-ups by doing more repetitions. Some players even devise a safe way to add weight on their backs for more resistance. Or make the exercise more difficult by going lower. Place soccer balls under both hands to be able to lower the body farther to improve strength. The balance required when using two balls is considerable.

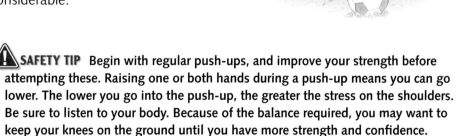

⚠ **SAFETY TIP** Begin with regular push-ups, and improve your strength before attempting these. Raising one or both hands during a push-up means you can go lower. The lower you go into the push-up, the greater the stress on the shoulders. Be sure to listen to your body. Because of the balance required, you may want to keep your knees on the ground until you have more strength and confidence.

Stability Ball Push-Up

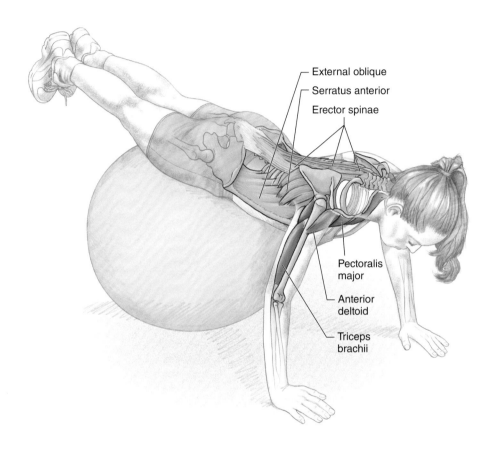

External oblique
Serratus anterior
Erector spinae

Pectoralis major

Anterior deltoid

Triceps brachii

Execution

1. Lie facedown on a stability ball. Lean forward, placing your hands on the floor.
2. Walk your hands forward until the ball is under your trunk, thighs, or feet. The exercise is more challenging the farther the ball is from your hands.
3. Get into the up push-up position with your hands on the floor, and perform routine push-ups.

Muscles Involved

Primary: Pectoralis major (especially clavicular portion), triceps brachii, anterior deltoid

Secondary: Serratus anterior, abdominal core and spinal extensors for proper posture

Soccer Focus

Strength and conditioning coaches have an arsenal of schemes to ensure that virtually every portion of any muscle can be exercised. A standard method is to change the alignment of the body in relation to the direction the resistance is being moved. In this case, the athlete tilts the body in a different way. Raising the legs effectively changes the way the pectoralis major muscle is used. In a routine push-up, the lower two-thirds to three-quarters of the muscle is addressed. Raising the legs brings the remaining upper portion of the pectoralis major muscle into the exercise.

VARIATIONS

This simple exercise has numerous variations. Using the stability ball, you can do a routine push-up with the feet on the floor and the hands squeezing the top and side of the ball. Or keep the hands on the ball, and prop your feet on a bench of the same height as the stability ball. Or leave the feet on the floor, and do push-ups with a stability ball for each hand. Also try this with the ball-height bench. Want a real challenge? Do push-ups with your feet on one ball and your hands on another. Or forget the balls altogether; keep the bench and do push-ups, placing the feet on the bench and the hands on the floor.

Bench Press

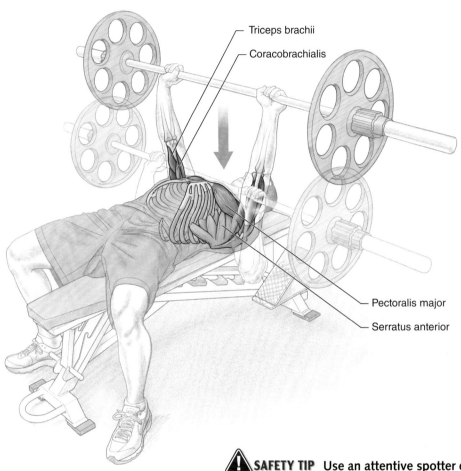

Triceps brachii

Coracobrachialis

Pectoralis major

Serratus anterior

⚠ SAFETY TIP Use an attentive spotter during this exercise for safety. Lock your thumbs around the bar. If you don't and lose control of the bar, the weight could slip out of your hand.

Execution

1. Lie on your back on a weight bench of sufficient length to support the body from the buttocks to the shoulders, with your feet flat on the floor. The barbell is on a rack at about nipple level.

2. Grasp the bar using an overhand grip, with the arms about shoulder-width apart.

3. With the arms extended but not locked at the elbows, lift the bar off the rack and stabilize the weight. There may be a little arching of the back at this point.

4. Lower the weight to the chest, pause briefly, and then extend the arms to lift the weight again. Keep the arms steady to support the weight, but do not lock the elbows. Inhale as you lower the bar, and exhale as you the press the bar up (blow the weight up).

Muscles Involved

Primary: Pectoralis major, triceps brachii, anterior deltoid

Secondary: Serratus anterior, coracobrachialis

Soccer Focus

In a crowded penalty area, positioning for a corner is less about pulling the opponent toward you than it is pushing the opponent away to increase the space around you. Exercises such as push-ups and bench presses are very helpful. In essence, a bench press is an upside-down push-up and recruits many of the same muscles. The major difference is that the barbell bench press is overloaded because of the added weight on the bar. This type of incremental increase in resistance for a push-up is not as simple.

Machine Chest Press

Most fitness clubs and weight rooms have both machines and free weights that can be used for a chest press. The machines are designed for safety. Machines that mimic a bench press can be supine, on which you lie on your back, or seated. They can also be simple (chest flys that do not use the triceps) or compound (using both the pecs and the triceps, such as a bench press).

To change the muscular emphasis of this exercise, you have many options—arch the back slightly, lift the feet off the floor, increase or decrease the width of the grip, create an incline, change the contact point on the trunk, and so on.

Dumbbell Pullover

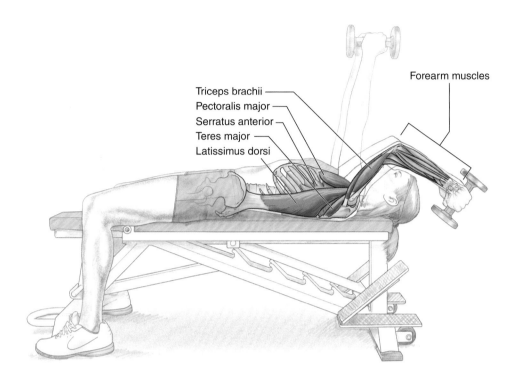

Triceps brachii
Pectoralis major
Serratus anterior
Teres major
Latissimus dorsi
Forearm muscles

⚠️ **SAFETY TIP** Have a partner put the dumbbell in your hands once you are lying on the bench.

Execution

1. Lie on your back on a weight bench of sufficient length to support your body from the buttocks to the shoulders, with your feet flat on the floor.
2. Wrap both hands around the inside weight of a dumbbell. Hold your arms extended and perpendicular to the floor.
3. Lower the dumbbell over your head and down, slightly bending the elbows.
4. After a slight pause, reverse the action and return to the starting position.

Muscles Involved

Primary: Latissimus dorsi, pectoralis major, triceps brachii, teres major

Secondary: Scapular stabilizers (rhomboid major and minor, trapezius, serratus anterior), forearm muscles (mostly wrist and finger flexors including flexor carpi radialis and ulnaris, palmaris longus, flexor digitorum superficialis and profundus, and flexor pollicis longus) to grasp dumbbell

Soccer Focus

Over the years, soccer players have become bigger and more athletic. This increase in size has changed the game on a number of fronts. For example, the modern goalkeeper can routinely punt a ball to the other goalkeeper on one bounce, and a 70-yard (64 m) goal kick by a professional male player is common. Another aspect that has changed is the throw-in. In earlier generations, a defender would try very hard to send the ball over the touchline (sideline) rather than give up a corner because a throw-in to the face of the goal was very unusual, while a corner was much more dangerous. Today, most teams have one or two designated throw-in specialists just for restarts near the end line. These specialists can deliver a throw that is more like a corner kick, giving the team another offensive weapon. The movement of the dumbbell pullover is very similar to a throw-in, and you can bet a team's throw-in specialist does this exercise. The poor defender now doesn't know where to send the ball (but most everyone would still rather face a throw than a corner).

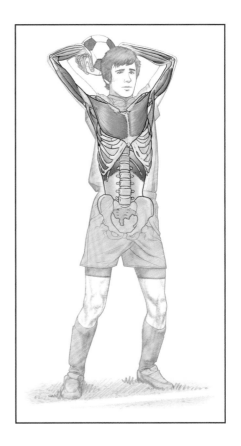

V A R I A T I O N

Machine Pullover

As with most free weight exercises, there are machine options that place the user in a fixed and safe position. Many of these machines are simple, isolating a single action such as the pullover motion, instead of compound, which allow actions across multiple joints.

Cable Crossover Fly

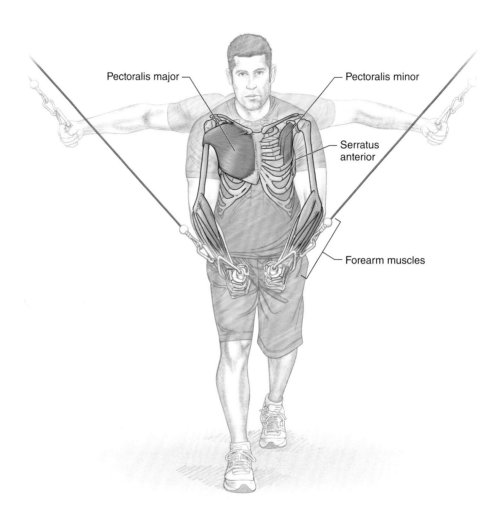

Pectoralis major

Pectoralis minor

Serratus anterior

Forearm muscles

Execution

1. This exercise usually requires a setup dedicated to this specific lift. Stand with your back to the weights. Stand with your feet staggered, with the trunk leaning a little bit forward.

2. Reach up behind you, and grasp the handles of the cable machine in an overhand grip. The arms will be extended behind you, with a little flexion at the elbows. Picture a bird opening its wings.

3. Inhale and squeeze the arms together in unison until the hands touch. Exhale when the hands touch. Try not to change the angle of elbow flexion during the movement.

4. Slowly allow the arms to return to the starting position. Be sure to keep control during the lift. It is easy to let gravity take over.

Muscles Involved

Primary: Pectoralis major, pectoralis minor

Secondary: Forearm muscles to grasp handles, scapular stabilizers (serratus anterior, rhomboid major and minor, middle trapezius)

Soccer Focus

One could argue soccer players use strength training strictly to supplement their soccer-specific training. In this case, a player could get by with a few compound exercises that train most muscles of the shoulders and arms. But just because a muscle performs a certain action doesn't mean the entirety of the muscle is being exercised. For example, the common bench press doesn't exercise a significant portion of the upper pectoralis major. Thus, a complete supplemental strength training program will include a variety of exercises to affect as many muscle fibers as possible. While the cable crossover fly is a great option that recruits most of the pectoralis major, it is also a great option to activate the pectoralis minor. The pectoralis minor lies under the pectoralis major and inserts on the scapula under the general area of origin of the deltoid. It stabilizes the scapula during movement. A stable scapula is important not only for optimal shoulder function but also to protect the shoulder when landing after a fall. This lift moves the scapula around the curvature of the ribs, which is a specific action of the pectoralis minor.

Pec Fly

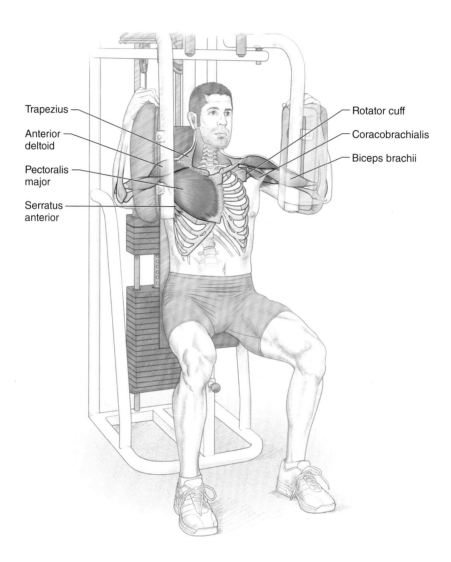

Trapezius

Anterior deltoid

Pectoralis major

Serratus anterior

Rotator cuff

Coracobrachialis

Biceps brachii

Execution

1. Make appropriate adjustments to the seat so that your upper arms are roughly parallel to the floor.
2. Open your arms and flex your elbows.
3. Place your elbows and forearms on the pads, and grasp the handles with an overhand grip. You do not need to hold the handles tightly.
4. Squeeze your arms together, pause briefly, and then return to the starting position.

Muscles Involved

Primary: Pectoralis major, coracobrachialis, anterior deltoid

Secondary: Scapular stabilizers, rotator cuff (subscapularis, supraspinatus, infraspinatus, teres minor), biceps brachii

Soccer Focus

This exercise is another option for the major chest muscles. Many athletes mistakenly believe that supplemental exercises should be specific to the sport and devise ways to mimic game actions using some form of resistance. There are many situations in soccer during which you can imagine the utility of some of these exercises, but pushing is probably not one of them. That should not be a reason to skip working the pectoral muscles. By undertaking a supplemental strength training program, you are making every attempt to improve your entire body, not just the specific movements of your sport. Exercises for the shoulders and back, which will help you maintain both your position and possession of the ball, must be balanced by exercises for the major chest muscles. An imbalance in strength between opposing muscles is a risk factor for joint injury, including injuries to the shoulder.

BACK AND HIPS

Undervaluing the importance of the back is very shortsighted when it comes to training. Nearly every functional movement in sports is anchored to the back. Some might say that because the back is not a location of many acute injuries in soccer, we don't need to worry about it. Although the back may not be injured very often, it might surprise some people to learn that about one-third of all male soccer players have complaints about their backs. This can range from just under 20 percent of local adult-league players to more than 50 percent of top-level players. In middle and high school players, back complaints were highest among those with the poorest skill, suggesting that one way to minimize back complaints might be to improve skill.

Back complaints may not be serious enough to cause a player to miss training or matches, but they can be irritating enough to catch the player's attention. Considering the torques around the body during kicking and cutting and the fact that something in the pattern of movement in soccer changes about every four to six seconds in terms of speed or direction, it should not be surprising to learn that these actions just might be culprits in the complaints expressed by players. And there is a growing body of evidence that pain, even pain not severe enough to keep an athlete out, might be the first warning of an impending overuse injury that could sideline a player for an extended period.

Physical therapists use many effective exercises to help strengthen the backs of people with chronic back pain. But the best treatment for chronic back pain is to prevent the pain before it starts—to stop the potential pain in its tracks before it becomes a complaint. A little bit of work done each day will show great benefits in the future. You don't need to start out with terribly challenging exercises, so take your time and you'll experience results fairly quickly. The more you have to gain, the more you will gain. Since most athletes have ignored their backs, they have a lot to gain. Vary your exercise choices, and don't overload this area, or any area, too frequently or intensely.

This chapter shows a number of exercises specifically for the back. A number of these options involve a ball or are a bit competitive so they can be fun. Others involve a partner, while a few are done in a gym.

Anatomy of the Vertebral Column

The back is made up of individual vertebrae and their cartilage, which make up the spinal column; ligaments for stability between each bone; the spinal cord, which carries information to and from your brain; and an almost dizzying array of muscles most players have never considered. In total, the back can be quite complicated. Consider the spinal cord. The spinal cord is more than just a series of highways carrying information to and from the brain. It is also capable of some decision making. As one spinal cord researcher recently said, "The brain gets things started, and the spinal cord sorts out the details."

The vertebral column is a series of similar bones. There are 7 cervical (neck), 12 thoracic (chest), and 5 lumbar vertebrae (figure 6.1, page 102). These are distinct and separate bones. Below this is the sacrum, which is made of 5 fused bones, and 3 to 5 coccygeal bones that may or may not be fused. The vertebral column is not arranged in a straight line. It has three curves within the sagittal plane that curve toward or away from the front of the body, not side to side. The cervical vertebrae curve anteriorly, the thoracic vertebrae curve posteriorly, and the lumbar vertebrae curve slightly anteriorly. The ribs articulate with the thoracic vertebrae.

Although the bones of each region have their own unique look, they all have the same common features. You see a large *body*, two lateral projections opposite each other (*transverse processes*), and a third projection by itself (*spinous process*) that all surround an opening (*vertebral foramen*) (figure 6.2); the anatomical term for a projection is a *process*, and a hole is a *foramen*. The large body is anterior, and the process opposite the body that is all by itself is posterior and points down. When you run your hand up and down someone's back, those bumps are the spinous processes. There are a number of bony contacts that by themselves allow for limited movement, but summed up allow the amazing movements of the entire column demonstrated by gymnasts, divers, acrobats, and dancers.

The vertebral foramen is for the spinal cord. When you put one vertebra on top of the other, another foramen (*intervertebral foramen*) is seen on each side, and this is where spinal nerves take information to and from the spinal cord. A large cartilaginous disc sits between the bodies of adjacent vertebrae. This disc has two distinct sections. The outer ring is called the annulus fibrosa and surrounds a gelatinous center, the nucleus pulposa (picture a jelly donut). A herniated disc is one that bulges out from between its vertebrae and can cause pain if the bulge pushes on the spinal cord or spinal nerves.

Each pair of vertebrae is connected by a series of short ligaments from the process above to the process below as well as other points of bony articulations. There are also long ligaments that run the length of the vertebral column. One ligament runs along the most anterior surface of each vertebral body, while an opposite ligament runs down the smooth

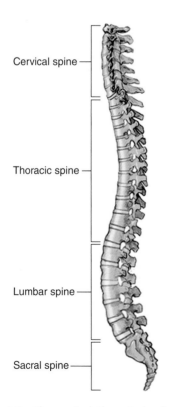

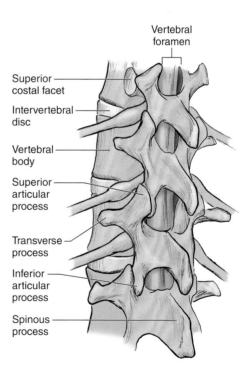

Figure 6.1   The cervical, thoracic, lumbar, and sacral regions of the spine.

Figure 6.2   The vertebrae of the spine.

posterior surface between the processes. A third ligament, the strongest of the three, the *ligamentum flavum*, runs the length of the posterior surfaces within the canal that houses the spinal cord. In total, these ligaments provide for impressive stability and mobility of the vertebral column.

The joints between each vertebra are complex and vary according to region and function. These joints can be capable of minimal movement, such as between the vertebral bodies, or can be quite movable, such as between the first and second cervical vertebrae to aid movements of the skull.

Back Muscles

The muscles of the spine are highly complex. There are long muscles that run the entire length of the vertebral column, and there are tiny muscles between each vertebra. Working individually or in groups, these muscles produce a wide range of movements. A number of back muscles with their origin on the vertebral column that attach to the scapula or arm are listed in chapter 4.

Spinal muscles differ from other muscles in that they don't really have a single origin or insertion. Most begin on the pelvis and insert along each vertebra up the column. Others begin on the vertebra below and insert on the vertebra above. Some have the opposite orientation, while still others overlap muscles up the column. Some are region specific, while others have segments both within and between sections.

The most widely recognized muscle acting on the vertebral column is the erector spinae (figure 6.3). This name is applied to a collection of muscles called the longissimus, spinalis,

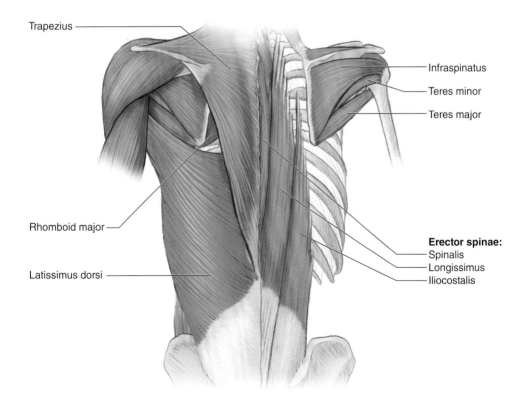

Figure 6.3 The muscles of the back.

and iliocostalis. Each of these may have region-specific portions, such as the semispinalis capitis, longissimus cervicis, and iliocostalis thoracis. As its name implies, the erector spinae extends the spine for an erect stance. Muscles pull the insertion toward the origin, so to extend the spine, the origins are low and the insertions are high on the back.

Other muscles of the back include the multifidus, quadratus lumborum, rotatores thoracis, and interspinalis. All told, there are about 30 pairs of named muscles that extend, rotate, compress, and perform lateral flexion of the various regions of the vertebral column.

Anatomy of the Hip

The pelvis, which makes up the hips, is actually three fused bones on each side (figure 6.4). The three bones are the ilium, ischium, and pubis. The configuration of the three bones can be confusing. That ridge you feel under the skin on your side is the fan-shaped crest of the ilium, or iliac bone. You sit on a specific landmark of your ischium. The two pubic bones connect with each other in the midline of the lower abdomen. These three bones are fused together, and each fused set of three bones connects with its counterpart on the other side through the pubic bones. Posteriorly, the two iliac bones articulate with each side of the sacrum to form the sacroiliac joint, a joint with surprisingly little motion.

Along with the pelvic floor muscles, the pelvis provides support from below for the abdominal organs, numerous locations for muscle attachment, passageways for nerves and blood vessels, and the site of bony articulation with the lower extremities. Injuries to this strong set of bones are not common, but there are a number of injuries to tissues that have some connection with the pelvic girdle.

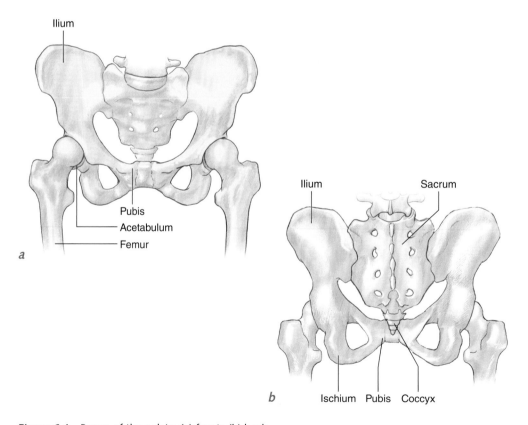

Figure 6.4　Bones of the pelvis: *(a)* front; *(b)* back.

Hip Muscles

The primary actions at the hip are flexion and extension. For hip flexion, bend your knee and raise it toward your trunk. Hip extension is the opposite motion; you move your leg behind your trunk.

Two sets of muscles create hip flexion. The primary muscles are part of a group called the iliopsoas. This group includes three muscles—the iliacus, psoas major, and psoas minor—that begin on the lower lumbar vertebrae and the deep cut of the pelvis. (Actually, half of people don't have the psoas minor muscle.) All insert through a common tendon on the femur to flex the hip and externally rotate the femur. Each psoas muscle also assists in lateral flexion of the trunk. Secondary muscles for hip flexion are the rectus femoris, one of the four quadriceps muscles of the thigh (see page 149), and the sartorius. Although these muscles are secondary for hip flexion, they are no less important. The rectus femoris begins on the rim of the socket portion of the ball-and-socket hip joint and joins with the other three quadriceps muscles to eventually insert on the tibia just below the patella (kneecap). The rectus femoris is primarily a knee extensor, but because of its origin on the pelvis, it also is a hip flexor. The sartorius is a curious muscle that begins roughly in the area where one might suffer a hip pointer (anterior superior iliac spine) and then runs sort of diagonally down the medial thigh and inserts behind the tibia below the knee, giving it numerous actions: hip flexion, knee flexion, hip abduction, and lateral rotation of the hip. If you were to check the sole of your shoe to see if you stepped on gum, you would involve all the actions of the sartorius.

Hip extension also requires two groups of muscles. The three hamstring muscles (see page 150) originate near the bony prominences on which you sit (ischial tuberosities) and insert below the knee on the back of the tibia and fibula. Their main function is knee flexion, but the pelvic attachment means they also perform hip extension. The other main muscle is the gluteus maximus, the large muscle of the buttocks. This very powerful muscle has a broad origin along the back of the pelvis and narrows to insert on the back of the proximal end of the femur. Because of the diagonal direction of its fibers, the gluteus maximus also can rotate the femur laterally as well as assist in trunk extension.

The other two gluteal muscles, the gluteus medius and the gluteus minimus, are named for their relative size and position. These originate underneath the gluteus maximus on the back of the pelvis but insert elsewhere on the femur to assist in thigh abduction (moving the thigh away from the midline of the body) and lateral thigh rotation. Depending on the position of the femur, the gluteus minimus also can help rotate the femur internally.

Prone Partner Ball Toss

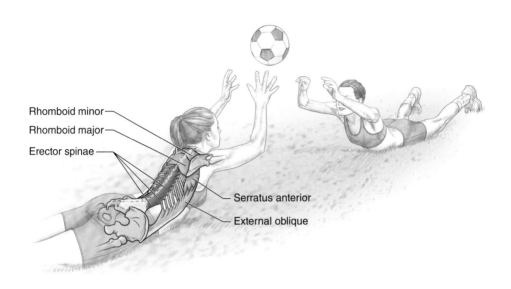

Rhomboid minor
Rhomboid major
Erector spinae
Serratus anterior
External oblique

Execution

1. You will need a partner for this exercise. Lie on your abdomen on the ground a few yards or meters away from your partner, head to head.
2. Take a soccer ball, arch your back to lift your chest off the ground, and gently toss the ball to your partner using both arms equally. Think of a throw-in.
3. Your partner arches her back to catch the ball. She tosses the ball back to you.
4. Continue tossing the ball back and forth. Toss back and forth for about 15 seconds, and add time as strength improves.

Muscles Involved

Primary: Erector spinae

Secondary: Abdominal core (external oblique, internal oblique, transversus abdominis, rectus abdominis), scapular stabilizers (such as rhomboid major and minor and serratus anterior)

Soccer Focus

We are learning more about the role of the spine in sport. Its role in the concept of the core should not be minimized, partly because we now know that some injuries to the lower extremity frequently are preceded by some minor wobble of the trunk. Add to this that a substantial percentage of soccer players have back complaints. These complaints may be enough to mention to the medical staff but not enough to keep the players off the field. The constant starting, stopping, and changing of direction in soccer twist the spine over and over again, which can lead to discomfort. Do not neglect supplemental training of the neck and spine just because you think such exercises are not soccer specific. Strengthening the muscles that attach to the spine will go a long way toward stabilizing the core, preventing injury, and minimizing back complaints. Although prone back extensions can be done individually, having the players toss a ball engages teammates with each other.

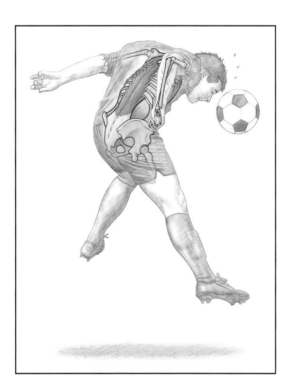

Seated Partner Ball Twist

Rectus abdominis
External oblique
Internal oblique

Erector spinae

Execution

1. You will need a partner for this exercise. Sit on the ground back to back with your partner. You may either extend or bend your legs for balance.
2. Hold a soccer ball in both hands.
3. At the same time, you and your partner twist to one side, and your partner reaches around to take the ball. Then you both twist to the opposite side, and your partner hands off the ball to you. Keep repeating the exercise for around 15 seconds, increasing the time as strength improves.

Muscles Involved

Primary: Abdominal core

Secondary: Spinal extensors (erector spinae, multifidus)

Soccer Focus

Soccer players are known for being among the most agile of all athletes. Agility is defined as being able to change speed, direction, and level quickly and accurately. The process of changing direction usually involves making a feint to get the opponent to move in one direction and then going off in another direction yourself. This feint is most effective if a twisting trunk is used to help decoy the opponent. The opponent will assume the rest of the body will follow the direction of the trunk. (An old coaching adage is to watch the numbers on the jersey in the belief they will tell you where the opponent is going.) Highly skilled and devious players know this and will use the trunk to confuse the defender. This exercise is good not only as part of a core training program but also to help a player's movements become harder to read. As players get better at this exercise, they will (usually on their own) try to do this drill faster and faster. In the gym, some swap out a soccer ball for a medicine ball, effectively adding resistance to the movement.

VARIATION

Broomstick Twist

The broomstick twist is a solo version of the partner exercise just described. The broomstick twist, a fundamental exercise in golf, requires only a stick of some kind. Try not to generate too much momentum. Perform the twist under control, with the goal of extending the limits of the trunk's range of motion, not to see how fast the movement can be performed.

Reach-Through Tug of War

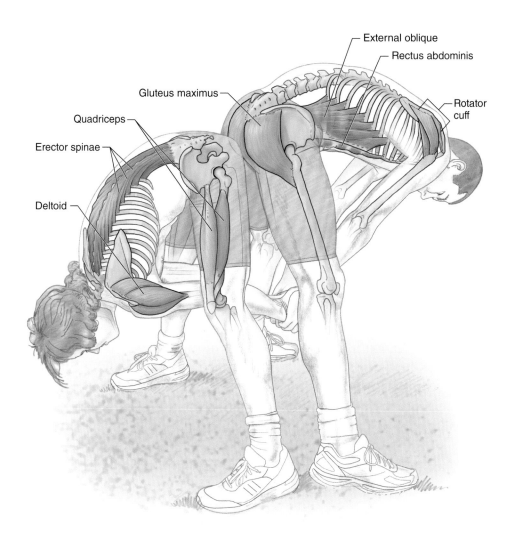

External oblique

Rectus abdominis

Gluteus maximus

Rotator cuff

Quadriceps

Erector spinae

Deltoid

Execution

1. You will need a partner for this exercise—one who is roughly your equal in size and strength. Stand back to back with your partner, both of you assuming a fairly wide stance.

2. Lean forward and reach through your legs, grasping both of your partner's hands.

3. On a "go" signal, try to pull your partner off balance as he tries to pull you off balance.

4. Break, pause for a few seconds, and repeat.

Muscles Involved

Primary: Rectus abdominis, external oblique, and internal oblique for trunk flexion; erector spinae for spinal extension

Secondary: Forearm muscles (mostly wrist and finger flexors including flexor carpi radialis and ulnaris, palmaris longus, flexor digitorum superficialis and profundus, and flexor pollicis longus) to grasp and hold hands; rotator cuff and other shoulder muscles (such as deltoid, rhomboid major and minor, levator scapulae, and serratus anterior) to maintain integrity of shoulder joint; larger hip and thigh muscles including gluteals (gluteus maximus, medius, and minimus), quadriceps (vastus medialis, vastus lateralis, vastus intermedius, rectus femoris), hamstrings (biceps femoris, semitendinosus, semimembranosus) and gastrocnemius to maintain balance, maintain standing position, and help pull on partner

Soccer Focus

This drill can be found in coaching books dating back to the 1950s and 1960s. It is very effective as a dynamic means of working trunk flexion and extension as well as balance and coordination of the trunk and spine along with the upper and lower extremities. Young players find the combination of the exercise and the competitiveness a fun way to test each other. As with other competitive exercises, players can get carried away with trying to overpower their partners and win the exercise.

On one level, this functional drill works the trunk and spine. On another level, it is a total-body exercise that requires balance, coordination, strength, and if performed long enough, some local muscle endurance, all good things for a game such as soccer.

Stability Ball Trunk Extension

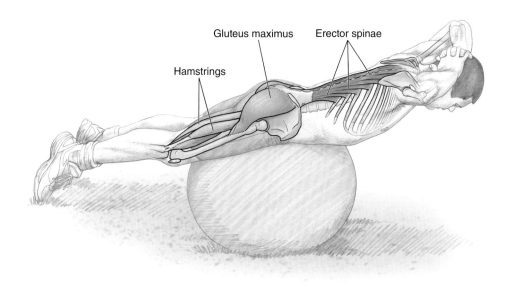

Gluteus maximus

Erector spinae

Hamstrings

Execution

1. Lean forward and place your hips on the stability ball, keeping your feet on the ground. Continue to lean forward, wrapping your trunk over the ball. Clasp your fingers behind your head.
2. Raise your chest off the ball, keeping the chin tucked in to stabilize the neck.
3. Slowly return to the starting position.

Muscles Involved

Primary: Erector spinae

Secondary: Trapezius, rhomboid major and minor, gluteus maximus, hamstrings

Soccer Focus

Acute, traumatic injury to the spine is, thankfully, rare in soccer. But that does not mean a soccer player's spine is immune to problems. When injury surveillance studies look beyond acute injury and ask players about any musculoskeletal complaints (things that bother them but do not prevent them from playing), back pain is cited by more than 50 percent of top-level adult players. And low back complaints are not just an issue for adult players—more than 40 percent of low-skilled youth players (14 to 16 years old) have low back complaints. Some researchers are investigating whether low-level

pain without a specific incident may be the first warning of an overuse injury such as a stress fracture. A spinal stress fracture would lead to an extended time-loss period, so athletes should do what they can to lessen the stresses on the spine in order to keep playing.

VARIATION

Oblique Crunch

You can increase the load on the obliques by doing stability ball crunches on your side and performing lateral flexion to the side opposite the ball.

Reverse Leg Extension

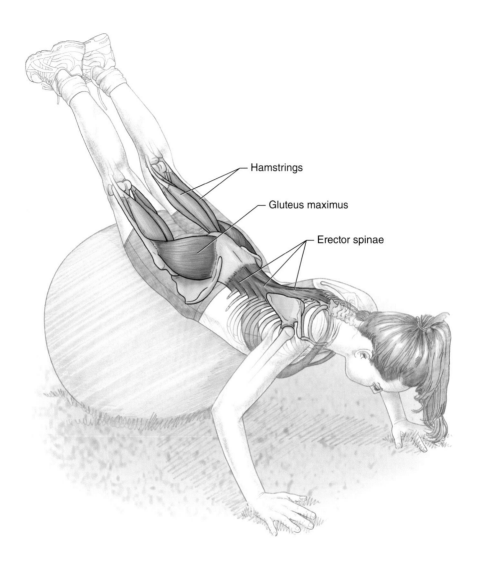

Hamstrings

Gluteus maximus

Erector spinae

Execution

1. Select a stability ball appropriate for your size: too big and you may not be able to touch the ground with the hands and feet at the same time; too small and there is little challenge.
2. Lie across the ball so that your lower abdomen is on the ball. Extend your arms, placing your palms on the ground. Your legs should be extended so that your toes touch the ground.
3. By extending your hips, raise both legs in unison as high as you can, keeping the legs straight.
4. Slowly return to the starting position.

Muscles Involved

Primary: Gluteus maximus, erector spinae

Secondary: Hamstrings

Soccer Focus

Heading is a hard skill to master. Those who are good at it are highly prized members of a team. When standing, it should be obvious that much of your heading power comes from pushing against the ground to provide the energy necessary for a successful heading opportunity. When jumping, you don't have the ground to push against, meaning you need to coordinate the hyperextension of your trunk with a rapid flexion of the trunk to apply power to the ball. In a match, this opportunity might happen only a couple of times, but heading practice (for appropriately aged players) can provide multiple opportunities for this hyperextension–flexion motion and the spinal muscles. Exercises that recruit the erector spinae muscles will help support the vertebrae during this demanding skill.

Partner Lumbar Extension

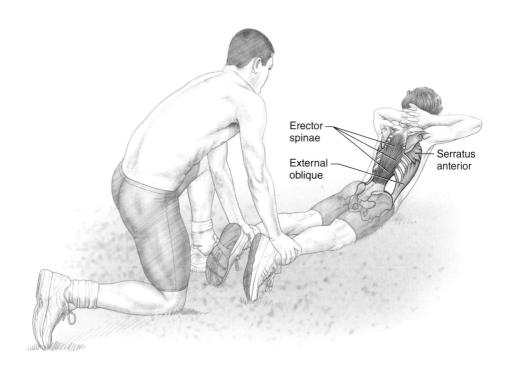

Erector spinae

External oblique

Serratus anterior

Execution

1. You will need a partner for this exercise. Lie supine on the ground, and clasp your hands behind your head. Your partner kneels at your feet and anchors your ankles to the ground.

2. Slowly extend your spine, raising your trunk and shoulders off the ground.

3. With control, lower the trunk to the ground and repeat. Do not go overboard at the beginning by attempting too many repetitions or trying to extend too far. Start with a few repetitions, and gradually add more.

4. Swap positions with your partner.

Muscles Involved

Primary: Erector spinae

Secondary: Abdominal core, rhomboid major and minor, serratus anterior, lower trapezius

Soccer Focus

Forceful kicking requires hyperextension of the back at the end of the preparatory phase. Note the degree of both hip and trunk hyperextension when preparing to kick the ball powerfully. This could happen more frequently in training or a match than what is seen during a powerful header. Add to this the very real chance that there will be some angular torque on the spine when approaching the ball from an angle, like a field goal kicker in American football. You probably have never appreciated the level to which your back is involved in soccer.

VARIATION

Rotating Lateral Extension

This variation includes the obliques in the exercise. Simply perform the exercise as described, only alternate a twist to each side with each repetition. As you get stronger, you might attempt to twist in both directions on each repetition.

Inclined Lumbar Extension

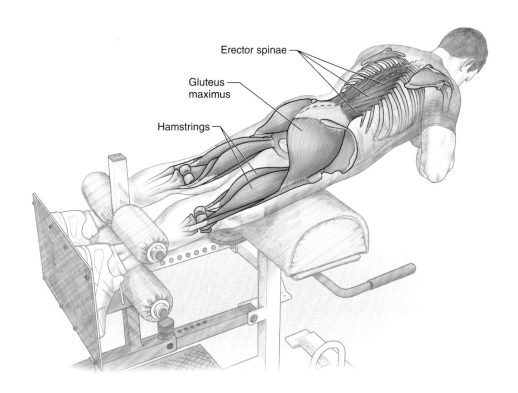

Erector spinae

Gluteus maximus

Hamstrings

Execution

1. Get into a prone position on a Roman chair by standing on the platform so that you can hook your ankles under the pads. Your thighs will be on the cushion and your arms folded across the chest. The hips need to be free to move.
2. Slowly lower the trunk to the floor.
3. Raise the trunk until it is in line with the legs.
4. Do not attempt too many repetitions. Start with a few, and gradually add more repetitions as you get stronger.

Muscles Involved

Primary: Erector spinae

Secondary: Gluteus maximus, hamstrings

Soccer Focus

A recent study looked at stress fractures to a particular area of the lumbar spine in young players. The name of the injury is a mouthful: spondylolysis (pronounced spon-de-LOL-eh-sis).The exact cause is still under study, whether it begins with a specific event or if there is a genetic component. Axial loading (pushing down on top of the bones) or repetitive twisting motions have both been suggested as potential culprits. Axial loading is not all that common in soccer, but excessive twisting is quite common. Rest is the best treatment for this condition, and most physicians expect three months or more lost to sport for complete healing. Most sports medicine specialists believe that increasing the strength of the muscles around susceptible bones and joints will go a long way toward preventing problems. This is especially true for the back, an area with a reputation for being weak and poorly conditioned.

Good Morning

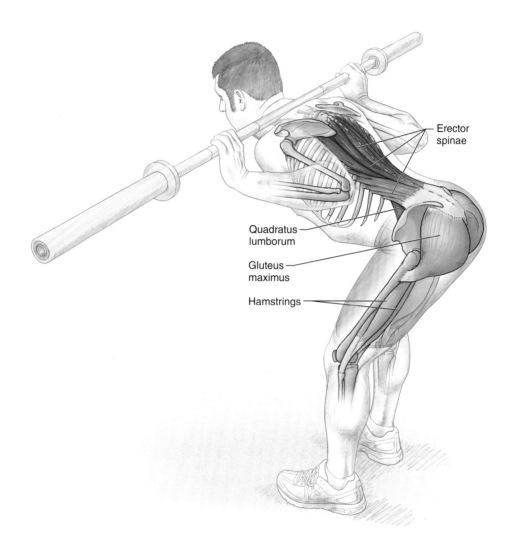

Erector
spinae

Quadratus
lumborum

Gluteus
maximus

Hamstrings

⚠ SAFETY TIP There is no need to use heavy weights for the exercise. A
slight bend at the knees can make this exercise a bit easier.

Execution

1. Stand with your feet apart, with a little knee flexion. Using an overhand
   grip, hold a barbell across your trapezius.
2. Slowly bend the trunk forward, while keeping the trunk straight and your
   head up, until the angle between the trunk and thigh is about 90 degrees.
3. Pause at the bottom, and then slowly raise the trunk.

Muscles Involved

Primary: Erector spinae, quadratus lumborum

Secondary: Gluteus maximus, hamstrings

Soccer Focus

Most of the examples so far have been directed toward field players. The goalkeeper has a unique position. The goalie spends a great deal of time apart from the action, talking to his defenders about positioning and opponent movements that might not be seen by all. More important, the goalie will usually need to make three or more saves to keep his team in the game. These actions are highly ballistic and frequently quite acrobatic and can bring gasps from spectators and players alike. Stretching across the goal mouth, arching his back, and reaching out to get his fingertips on the ball to redirect the shot away from danger requires every muscle to be prepared to act in an instant. Because the goalie also is allowed to use his hands, his upper trunk and upper body have a unique role in comparison with field players. Goalies are getting bigger, with players 6 feet 2 inches (188 cm) or taller routinely manning the posts. Just the length of a goalie this size changes the torque about his joints.

VARIATION

Machine Back Extension

Machines offer a safe and stable way to isolate a muscle group. Athletes with a history of back pain or back complaints as well as athletes returning from injury should use a back extension machine as their first choice.

CHAPTER 7

ABDOMEN

On many levels, the old guys were right about a great many things about soccer coaching. Drills that seem novel today often can be found in coaching books from decades ago. Just because someone coached in the 1950s or 1960s doesn't mean he didn't know the game. Although we have revised their recommendations for fluid replenishment and distance running for match fitness, their thoughts on individual ball training are being revisited as coaching methods go through inevitable cycles. Coaches of a generation or two ago would have players do sit-ups to strengthen their abdominals to withstand collisions. Today, most people, athletes included, will point to their abdominals when asked about their core, probably saying something about six-pack abs. In reality, the core is far more than just the abdominal muscles. The core refers to the body's midsection from the hips to the shoulders. Around this center, all movements occur.

A strong core is the platform around which your limbs perform. For the upper and lower extremities to move about the trunk in the most coordinated manner, the muscles of the core, of which the abdominals are just one part, need to stabilize the hips, spine, and trunk. If the trunk is not stable during movement, the limbs will have to compensate for unexpected movements by the trunk. To demonstrate this, stand on one leg, close your eyes, and note what happens to the lifted leg and your arms as your trunk shifts away from being over the support leg. Reactions like this in the frantic, uncontrolled situations of a match might lead to something unfavorable, such as an injury. In fact, high-speed videos of people who experienced noncontact knee injuries show that just before the injury the trunk wavered slightly, the player reacted a little differently than planned, and the knee failed. This is why core training is part of almost every knee injury prevention program, such as The 11+ (see chapter 2, page 18).

Over time, the core has gone from being a training afterthought ("a few sit-ups") to being a key—some might say *the* key—element in a training program. Because of the dozens of books, hundreds of exercise options, and thousands of websites devoted to core training, choosing training options can be intimidating.

The lower abdomen, between the rib cage and the pelvis, is like a cylinder. At its sides are the abdominal muscles, the spinal muscles, and the lumbodorsal fascia. The diaphragm above and the pelvic floor below close the ends of the cylinder.

Abdominal Muscles

The abdomen is unique in that the skeletal structure for muscle attachments is borrowed from other regions of the body. From above, some abdominal muscles originate on the ribs, and from below, others originate from the pelvis. From the back, still other muscles originate from the vertebral column and a very strong layer of tendinous tissue in the lower back called the lumbodorsal fascia (sometimes called the thoracolumbar fascia). Because of the limited locations for bony insertion for the lower abdominal muscles, portions of the muscles that wrap around the front attach to a tendon called the *linea alba* that runs from the sternum to the pelvis. This gives certain muscles an attachment to pull on. There are few traditional joints or ligaments in the abdomen. The structure of the pelvis is outlined in chapter 6.

The most obvious muscles of the abdomen are the transversus abdominis, external oblique, and internal oblique (figure 7.1). Their arrangement and functions are complex. These three muscles are flat sheets that lie one on top of another. They are named for the direction of their fibers and their location in the layers. A fourth muscle, the rectus abdominis, is embedded within the midline tendons in what is called the rectus sheath.

The paired rectus abdominis muscles run side by side and adjacent to the midline, between the sternum and pubic bones, the lowest part of the abdomen. The rectus abdominis originates where the two pubic bones join (the pubic symphysis). The fibers run up to the end of the sternum (the xiphoid process) and the nearby surfaces of the 5th through 7th ribs. This muscle

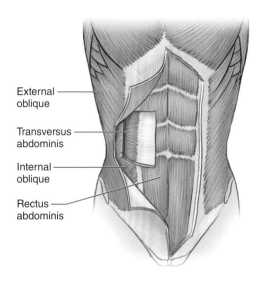

Figure 7.1   Transversus abdominis, external oblique, internal oblique, and rectus abdominis.

is unique in that there are tendons within the muscle. In most cases, a tendon is the link between a muscle and a bone, but the rectus abdominis has three tendons that break the muscle into distinct sections. When this muscle is well trained and the layer of fat under the skin is thin, the result is the highly sought after six-pack appearance associated with rock-hard abs.

The external oblique, as its name implies, is the outermost layer of the abdominal muscles that wrap around the lower abdomen. Its fibers run in a diagonal direction. It originates laterally on the outer surface of the lower 8 ribs, and the fibers run diagonally *down* toward the pelvis to insert on the iliac crest (that bony ridge on your side), the rectus sheath, and the linea alba.

The internal oblique lies just under the external oblique, and their fibers run perpendicular to each other. The internal oblique originates from the lumbodorsal fascia of the lower back and the adjacent iliac crest of the pelvis. Its fibers run diagonally *up* to the outer surfaces of the 9th through 12th ribs, the rectus sheath, and the linea alba.

The deepest abdominal muscle is the transversus abdominis. This muscle has a broad area of origin from the outer, lateral surface of the lower 6 ribs, the lumbodorsal fascia, and the iliac crest. Its fibers run horizontally to insert on the linea alba and rectus sheath. Don't make the mistake of calling this the transversus abdominal oblique. The fibers are horizontal, not diagonal, so to add *oblique* would contradict the *transversus* in its name.

These three muscles connect to the linea alba by way of fairly long, flat tendons because the actual muscle tissue ends well lateral of the midline. The only muscles per se that are on either side of the navel are the paired rectus abdominis muscles.

Many people believe the abdominals collectively perform trunk flexion and trunk rotation. But when considering the direction of the muscle fibers, it is as hard for the rectus abdominis to aid in rotation as it is for the transversus abdominis to perform trunk flexion.

Since we know the direction of the fibers, the attachments, and the rule about muscles pulling the insertion toward the origin, the actions of the abdominal muscles are predictable, if complex. Also remember that these muscles can work with their partners on the opposite side or work alone. Let's look first at the external oblique. When both external oblique muscles contract, they flex the trunk. When the muscle on the right side contracts, the trunk flexes laterally to the right. In addition, when the muscle on the right side contracts, the trunk can rotate toward the left.

The internal oblique is similar but has one main difference. Contract both sides to flex the trunk. Contract the muscle on the right side, and the trunk flexes laterally to the right. The difference is with rotation. Contract the muscle on the right side, and the trunk rotates to the right.

The transversus abdominis has different isolated actions. When activated, it increases intra-abdominal pressure and provides support for the abdominal organs.

The final abdominal muscle, the rectus abdominis, flexes the trunk and also helps perform lateral flexion and rotation.

Collectively, all four of these abdominal muscles work with each other and the long spinal muscles (see chapter 6) to provide support and stabilization for what many fitness professionals refer to as the lumbo–pelvic–hip complex.

The abdominals also play other roles. They contribute to the integrity of the vertebral column. In fact, weak abdominal muscles are often responsible for low back pain caused by poor intervertebral disc alignment. The abdominals also can aid in exhalation. When they contract, they squeeze on the underlying organs that push up against the diaphragm to increase intrathoracic pressure and help push air out of the lungs. And most people can appreciate the contribution of the abdominals in evacuating the bowels from the last time they had a lower gastrointestinal flu.

Those who choose to look further into abdominal exercises and core fitness will find dozens of exercises designed to activate very specific areas of the core such as the upper, middle, or lower abs. Such specificity will ensure that every aspect of each muscle is activated. It is easy to get both overwhelmed with the exercise options and carried away with implementing more activities at the expense of technical and tactical training for the game. Athletes are encouraged to perform their core training at a time apart from formal team training, reserving a few core exercises for the warm-up.

Reverse Crunch

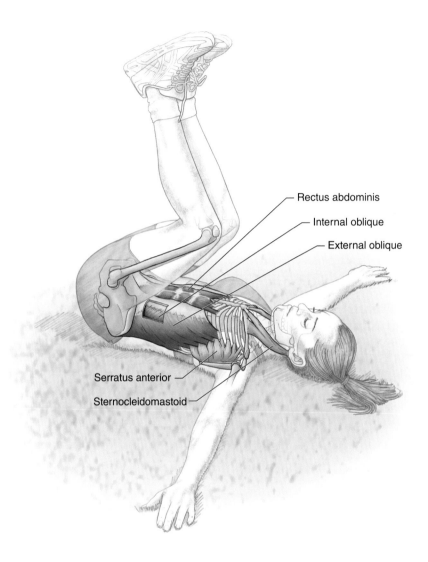

Rectus abdominis

Internal oblique

External oblique

Serratus anterior

Sternocleidomastoid

Execution

1. Lie on the ground on your back, and spread your arms to the sides for balance. Keep your head, neck, and shoulders on the ground.

2. Flex at the hips and knees, and raise the knees until they are over the hips.

3. Perform the crunch by pulling the knees in toward the head. Perform the exercise slowly. The primary movement is pulling the knees toward the head. Do not move the shoulders or head to the knees.

4. Pause and then return to the starting position.

Muscles Involved

Primary: Rectus abdominis, external oblique, internal oblique

Secondary: Sternocleidomastoid, serratus anterior, rhomboid major and minor, lower trapezius, psoas major and minor

Soccer Focus

A strong core is so important in sport for posture and general fitness, for performance and skill enhancement, and for injury prevention. A strong core anchors the movements of the limbs and minimizes extraneous motions often seen in players with poor technique. Much of the skill needed to play soccer involves rotation around an axis, and a strong core is the foundation for efficient movement. A strong core is also a factor in good posture. Muscles work best when the skeleton is properly aligned. A slouched posture increases the effort of the movement. Performance is enhanced when the body does not have to use unnecessary muscles to execute a movement. A strong core is known to have effects beyond the muscles to prevent injury. Some leg injuries, especially ligament injuries of the knee, are linked to a weak core that allows slight movements that need to be compensated for at the knee.

Soccer Ball Crunch

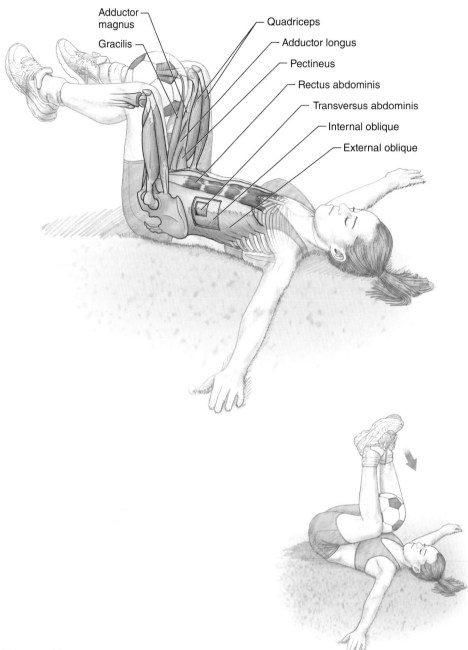

Adductor magnus
Gracilis
Quadriceps
Adductor longus
Pectineus
Rectus abdominis
Transversus abdominis
Internal oblique
External oblique

Execution

1. Lie on your back, arms stretched to the sides and knees bent with thighs perpendicular to the ground. Squeeze a soccer ball between your knees.

2. Pull your knees toward your chest by lifting your pelvis off the ground, trying to get your lower legs perpendicular to the ground.

3. Slowly return your hips and legs to the starting position.

Muscles Involved

Primary: Rectus abdominis

Secondary: External oblique, internal oblique, transversus abdominis, quadriceps (vastus medialis, vastus lateralis, vastus intermedius, rectus femoris), hip flexors (psoas major and minor, iliacus), adductors (adductor magnus, adductor longus, adductor brevis, pectineus, gracilis)

Soccer Focus

Core training has gone from being an afterthought to being a primary focus of training. More than just the abdominal muscles, the core includes every muscle that crosses the body's center—muscles that work together to accelerate and decelerate almost every activity in all sports. Power developed in the lower extremities can diminish as the energy passes up the movement chain, so developing the core helps transfer power to the extremities for performance. Because soccer has many abrupt

changes in speed, direction, or both, a weak core could mean the trunk and upper limbs might react to changes in an uncontrolled manner, placing the lower limbs in a precarious position that could lead to injury. Awkward movements of the trunk have been reported to precede ACL injuries.

VARIATION

Captain's Crunch

Dozens of exercises are designed to strengthen the core. The soccer ball crunch can be performed on the field. A variation of this crunch focuses on the rectus abdominis and can be done in the weight room using a captain's chair. Support yourself on your forearms in the captain's chair, flex your knees, and lift your knees toward your chest.

Bicycle Crunch

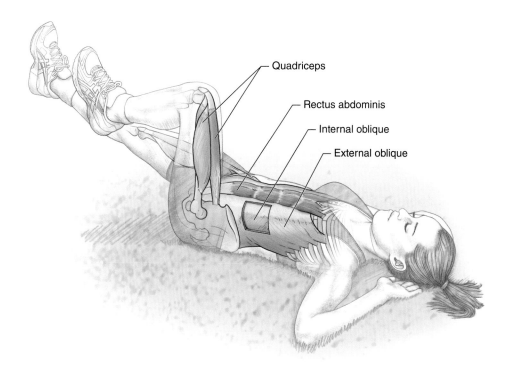

Execution

1. Lie on your back with your hands behind your head, fingers barely touching. The shoulders should be on the ground.

2. Draw one leg toward the chest so that the thigh is at about a 90-degree angle to the trunk. Draw the other leg up so that the thigh is at about a 45-degree angle to the trunk.

3. Alternate the legs back and forth as though you were riding a bicycle.

Muscles Involved

Primary: Rectus abdominis

Secondary: Hip flexors, quadriceps, adductors, external oblique, internal oblique

Soccer Focus

A number of core training exercises are performed in a slow, controlled manner. This exercise can be performed slowly or rapidly, depending on your goals. When this exercise is performed rapidly, the core is exposed to higher-velocity limb movements similar to those experienced during competition. Many experts suggest doing core training at high speed for just that reason. Increasing the speed of movement makes the exercise more functional and dynamic, which will help you prepare the core for those explosive and reactive balance situations that happen every four to six seconds. A strong core will help you transfer the power you've developed from performing the exercises in this book to the field of play.

VARIATION

Twisting Bicycle Crunch

To make the bicycle crunch more intense and increase the involvement of the external and internal obliques, bring the right elbow to the left knee and vice versa.

Vertical Leg Crunch

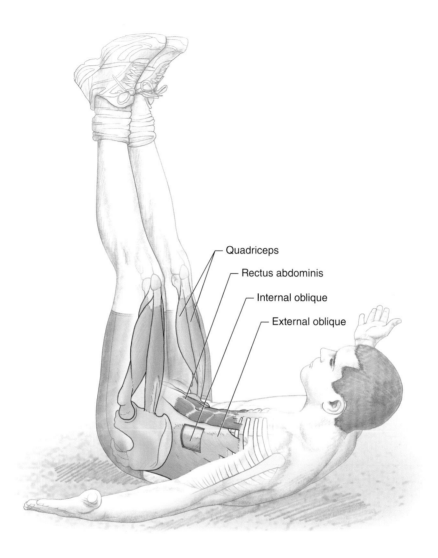

Quadriceps

Rectus abdominis

Internal oblique

External oblique

Execution

1. Lie on your back with your hands on the ground beside you.
2. Flex your hips to bring both legs vertical. You may prefer to cross your feet.
3. Slowly perform a crunch. Attempt to bring the sternum toward the thighs. Do not flex the neck.
4. Return to the starting position and repeat.

Muscles Involved

Primary: Rectus abdominis

Secondary: External oblique, internal oblique, hip flexors, quadriceps

Soccer Focus

A great deal of work has been done to determine which portions of the abdominals are used most in specific exercises. The general thought is that a routine crunch focuses mostly on the upper portion of the abdominals. When you lie back and flex the hips to raise your legs, the focus shifts toward the lower abdominals. Doing both types of crunches allows you to train a greater portion of the total abdominal mass. This is important when thinking about the transfer of power during the execution of skills. The buildup of kinetic energy for kicking begins when the planting foot strikes the ground. Power builds and is transferred up the leg through the abdomen and hips and then down the kicking leg. You can lose a lot of that power if the core fails to fully control the trunk, wasting some energy in unwanted trunk rotation or other movement. Engaging all the abs with the entire core fixes the trunk to allow the transfer of kinetic power from one link in the chain to the next. Although this is an abdominal exercise, you probably will experience some hip flexion. Try to keep your neck neutral by not letting your chin tuck toward your chest. For more resistance, hold a small medicine ball in your outstretched arms, and move the ball toward or beyond the feet as you crunch.

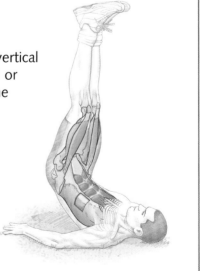

VARIATION

Full Vertical Crunch

This small variation changes the focus of the vertical leg crunch. Clasp the hands behind your head or to your sides for stability and perform a routine crunch, only this time push your feet toward the ceiling to give your body a U shape. This effectively shifts the focus from the rectus abdominis only and draws in more core muscles.

Single-Leg Abdominal Press

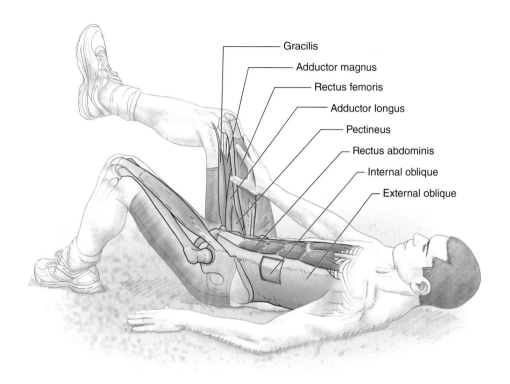

Gracilis

Adductor magnus

Rectus femoris

Adductor longus

Pectineus

Rectus abdominis

Internal oblique

External oblique

Execution

1. Lie on your back on the ground with your feet flat and your knees bent.
2. Raise your right leg so that both the knee and the hip are at a 90-degree angle.
3. Place your right hand on your thigh down near your knee.
4. Use your abdominals to further flex your trunk while resisting the movement with your hand.
5. Change to the left leg and repeat.

Muscles Involved

Primary: Rectus abdominis, psoas major and minor, iliacus

Secondary: Rectus femoris, adductors, external oblique, internal oblique

Soccer Focus

Although this is listed as an abdominal exercise, it is also an example of a field-based strength training exercise for hip flexion. Hip flexor strain injuries are becoming more common in soccer and, like hamstring strains, appear to result from the increased speed of the modern game. Strain injuries happen when a muscle contracts strongly when it has been lengthened. In sprinting, just before the trailing leg leaves the ground, the hip flexors are stretched. Once that foot leaves the ground, the hip flexes powerfully. This combination of stretch and contractile forces can tear the muscle. This can also happen when taking a hard kick, such as shooting or making a goal kick. There are about six muscles linked together as hip flexors, about half of which are classic groin muscles (adductors) that also assist with hip flexion. The other muscles, the rectus femoris (one of the four quadriceps), the iliopsoas, and the sartorius all perform hip flexion as a primary action. This exercise is designed to improve the strength of those main hip flexors. This should not, however, be the only method for preventing hip flexor strains. The walking lunge (page 34 in chapter 2) should also be performed at each training session to prevent this frustrating injury.

VARIATION

Opposite-Arm Abdominal Press

Using the opposite arm requires the trunk to twist, thereby increasing the use of the external and internal oblique muscles. In addition, this method also is thought to increase the use of a group of the lesser known, but very important, pelvic floor muscles, the levator ani and the coccygeus.

Stability Ball Trunk Lift

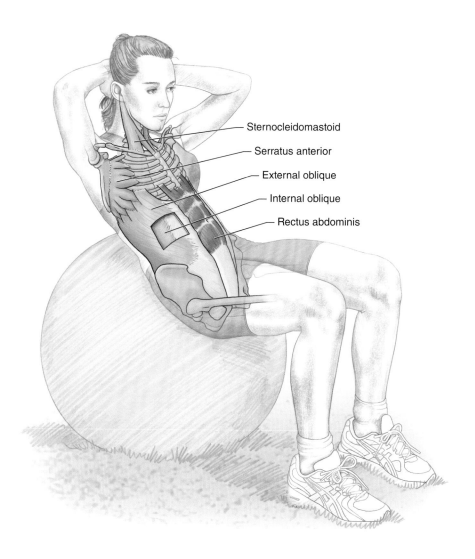

- Sternocleidomastoid
- Serratus anterior
- External oblique
- Internal oblique
- Rectus abdominis

Execution

1. Lie back across a large stability ball so that the ball is under your lower back. Your feet should be flat on the ground and spread to a comfortable distance that will help maintain stability. Your thighs should be parallel to the ground, and knees should be at 90 degrees of flexion. Lightly hold your fingers behind your head.

2. Using your abdominals, slowly raise your shoulders off the ball as far as you can. Keep the neck as straight as possible to avoid tucking your chin.

3. Pause at the top of the motion before slowly returning to the starting position.

Muscles Involved

Primary: Rectus abdominis

Secondary: External oblique, internal oblique, serratus anterior, sternocleidomastoid

Soccer Focus

Years ago, the emphasis on the core was probably limited to some sit-ups and maybe some straight-leg raises. Today, the role of the core has risen from almost an afterthought to a primary focus of training. Why is the core so important? Many fitness professionals believe that nearly all movement extends from the core and most certainly passes through the core. Thus, it is difficult to coordinate the lower and upper body with each other for efficient movement through a weak core. Inefficient movements through a weak core increase the risk of injury and may lead to hip instability that must be compensated for. This reactive compensation alters normal movement patterns and can cause injuries, with the knee being the weak link in this chain of events.

Practically every action in soccer—running, cutting, stopping, landing, kicking, and heading—can be performed more efficiently if you have a strong core.

VARIATION

Side-to-Side Trunk Lift

Hold a soccer ball in your hands, and add a twist to the movement to increase emphasis on the external and internal obliques. This simple variation increases the muscle mass for this exercise. Want to make this a bit harder? Use a medicine ball instead of a soccer ball. Medicine balls come in different weights. Hold a light medicine ball with your arms extended perpendicular from your trunk. Move up to progressively heavier medicine balls to increase the intensity of the exercise.

V-Sit Soccer Ball Pass

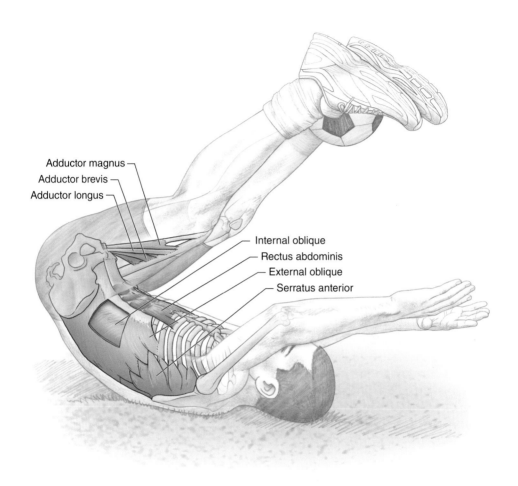

Adductor magnus
Adductor brevis
Adductor longus

Internal oblique
Rectus abdominis
External oblique
Serratus anterior

Execution

1. Lie on your back with your arms and legs extended. Clench a soccer ball between your ankles.

2. Keeping your legs straight, raise the ball over your head until the ball is over your hands, and then drop the ball into your hands. This is the first repetition.

3. Lower your feet to the starting position, leaving the ball in your hands.

4. Repeat the motion in order to retrieve the ball from the hands. This is the second repetition. At first, you may not be able to keep your legs straight throughout the exercise. As your strength improves, work on keeping the legs as straight as you can for as much of the exercise as possible.

Muscles Involved

Primary: Rectus abdominis

Secondary: External oblique, internal oblique, adductors, hip flexors, quadriceps, serratus anterior

Soccer Focus

This exercise has a long history in soccer and is described in many older coaching books. Back in the early 1970s, Pepsi partnered with the legendary Pele to produce the so-called Pepsi Pele movies that showed a number of his training methods. One of the movies featured a fitness circuit that had multiple stations for what might be considered early-generation core training. The exercises included basic sit-ups and what we eventually would call crunches. The films also showed Pele on the ground with a partner holding his ankles about waist high for a sort of inclined sit-up. The exercise that got everyone's attention was Pele lying on his back, his head between the feet of his partner and holding his partner's ankles. Pele raised his feet over his head to his partner's hands, and the partner then shoved Pele's feet toward the ground. Pele never allowed his feet to touch the ground. The audience usually groaned. Although most people would prefer exercises with less strain on the low back, one has to wonder how much of Pele's training contributed to his ability and longevity in the game. Most strength and conditioning coaches prefer to select a variety of core exercises rather than focus on just a few, as was done in the past. Doing too many repetitions of a few exercises can place unwanted stress on tissues, which can lead to overuse injury. Using the ball for some core work, such as this exercise, keeps players focused on the ball while doing the core a world of good.

Stability Ball Pike

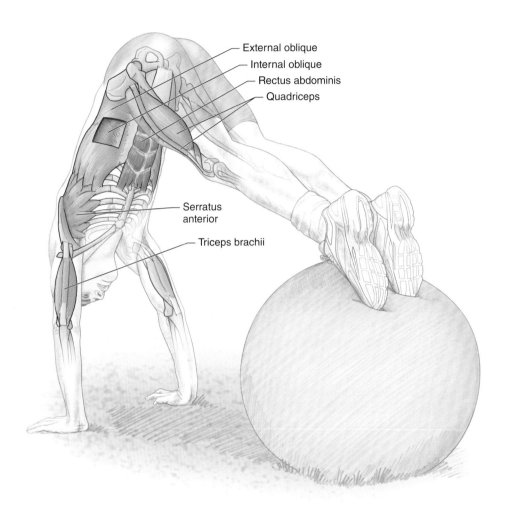

External oblique
Internal oblique
Rectus abdominis
Quadriceps

Serratus anterior

Triceps brachii

Execution

1. Get into an up push-up position with your shins on top of a large stability ball.

2. Flex to raise the hips while rolling the ball as far forward as possible from your shins to your toes. Make sure both your back and legs remain straight throughout the full movement.

3. Return to the starting position.

Muscles Involved

Primary: Rectus abdominis

Secondary: External oblique, internal oblique, serratus anterior, hip flexors, triceps brachii, quadriceps

Soccer Focus

A strong core is important for many reasons. Since your arms and legs extend from the trunk, it's only logical that a strong core will be an anchor for efficient movement of the limbs. In addition, forces for whole-body movements that are generated by the legs need to be transferred across the core to the arms for successful performance (e.g., when using the arms to make your trunk bigger when in a crowd of players maneuvering to receive a goal kick or a corner kick). When forces pass through a weak core, some of the force generated will be lost to other nonfunctional movements, meaning less force gets to its destination. The core is the link between the upper and lower body. The stronger the core, the less energy will be lost and the more force can pass between the upper and lower body for the most efficient movements.

Cable Crunch

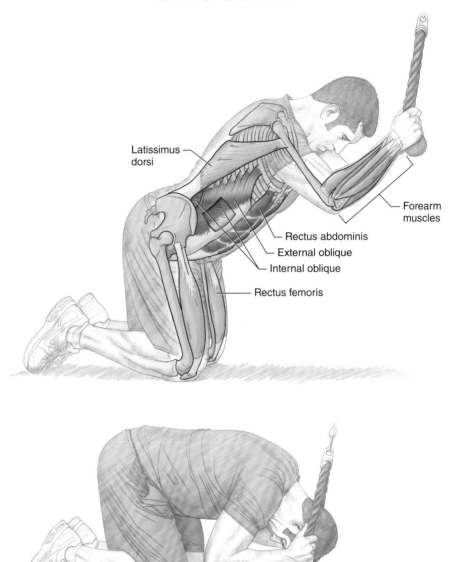

Latissimus dorsi

Forearm muscles

Rectus abdominis

External oblique

Internal oblique

Rectus femoris

Execution

1. Kneel in front of a cable machine, facing the weights.
2. Using an overhand grip, pull the rope attachment down to the shoulders and flex the hips slightly. (Your machine may have a long bar, short bar, handles, or a ropelike attachment to the cable.)
3. Inhale, and then exhale while crunching by rolling the sternum toward the pubis. Your elbows should move toward the middle of your thighs.
4. Slowly return to the starting position.

Muscles Involved

Primary: Rectus abdominis, external oblique, internal oblique

Secondary: Forearm muscles (mostly wrist and finger flexors, including flexor carpi radialis and ulnaris, palmaris longus, flexor digitorum superficialis and profundus, and flexor pollicis longus) to grasp rope, latissimus dorsi, rectus femoris, psoas major and minor

Soccer Focus

Most crunches are performed on the floor. This variation of a traditional crunch is performed from a kneeling position, and it takes a little practice to do the movement properly. The plus for this exercise is that you can increase the resistance by adding weight without having to figure out a way to hold a plate. As in all core exercises, draw in the core by pulling your navel toward your spine. You can also work the obliques by adding a slight twist during the crunch. Resist the temptation to do this exercise quickly, and you do not need to use heavy weights. Remember, this is an exercise for the abdominals, not for the hip flexors; use your abs.

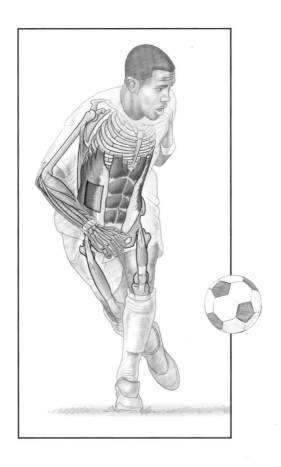

Hanging Hip Flexion

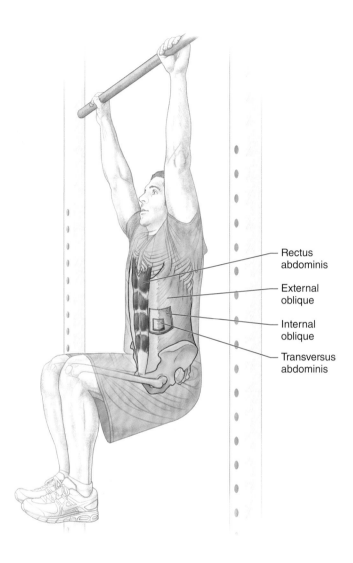

Rectus abdominis

External oblique

Internal oblique

Transversus abdominis

Execution

1. With an overhand grip, grasp a fixed overhead bar.
2. Flex the hips and knees until your thighs are parallel to the floor or higher.
3. Pause and then slowly return to the starting position.
4. Pause at the bottom before repeating to avoid generating any momentum. This exercise is about control, not about how fast you can do the exercise.

Muscles Involved

Primary: Rectus abdominis, hip flexors

Secondary: External oblique, internal oblique, transversus abdominis

Soccer Focus

This hanging exercise, like many other core exercises, involves a number of muscles. How it is done depends on what muscles are most active. For example, if the movement is just hip flexion and doesn't involve much flexion about the waist, the primary muscles are the hip flexors, and the abdominals act mostly as static stabilizers of the pelvis and waist. Raising the knees as high as possible recruits the rectus abdominis and the obliques, adding their dynamic contribution to the movement. You can add more oblique involvement by adding a slight twist to each side as you approach the end of each repetition. But don't think this exercise or any other abdominal exercise will reduce fat around the midsection. There is no proof that you can lose fat from one specific location (a process referred to as spot reduction).

At last, exercises for the legs. Maybe now you'll gain the strength for that killer shot, the 60-yard goal kick, or the accurate penetrating pass out of the back that shreds the defense. Soccer is primarily about the legs. All other exercises are for support. Let's get to the good stuff.

For most sports, the power behind the activity comes from the legs. Even sports that emphasize the arms build momentum from the ground up. Problems in the legs can affect the arms and shoulders. For example, the damaged shoulder of baseball pitching legend Jay Hanna Dean, better known as Dizzy Dean, began with a toe injury. A soccer player who does not have a good foundation may soon find a lack of balance, agility, and more affecting his soccer skills. Ill-timed or poorly executed actions above the legs can be seen as poor skill execution. Players who spend too much time working their legs while neglecting the rest of the body will never be the players others thought they could be.

Players make the greatest gains in developing a stronger shot or a longer goal kick by kicking. Improvements in velocity and distance are due mostly to the coordinated timing of all the complex mechanical actions of kicking with the recruitment of the optimal muscle fibers at the instant of ball contact. Improving strength improves general motor skill performance and prevents injury.

Bones, Ligaments, and Joints of the Legs

The leg is made up of three main bones. The femur (thigh bone) is above the tibia (shin bone), which is parallel to the fibula. The patella (knee cap) has no direct bony connection to the femur or tibia because it is embedded in the back of the tendon of the large thigh muscle, the quadriceps femoris. The foot and ankle are a complex mix of seven tarsals, five metatarsals, and 14 phalanges. Although the actions and dexterity of the foot are less than in the hand, the foot is no less complex.

The hip, knee, and ankle are the three primary joints of the leg, but there are more. The hip is the classic ball-and-socket joint. It is a very strong, sturdy joint whose integrity is supported by three very strong ligaments that begin on the pelvis and wrap around the neck of the femur. The hip has good range of motion, but not as good as the shoulder. The primary actions are flexion (swinging the thigh forward) and extension (swinging the thigh back), abduction (moving the leg sideways away from the body) and adduction (swinging the leg from the side back to the midline), internal rotation (rotating the thigh in toward the midline) and external rotation (rotating the thigh away from the midline), and circumduction (swinging the leg around in a circular motion).

The knee, where the femur sits on top of the flat surface of the tibia, is the definitive hinge joint. There is also the patellofemoral joint, where the patella glides along a smooth surface of the femur. The patella doesn't *attach* to the femur per se. Although the knee is a hinge joint like the fingers, it is a very complex joint. The real magic of the knee is in its ligaments. The medial collateral ligament, or MCL, connects the femur and tibia on the medial side of the knee, between the knees. The lateral collateral ligament, or LCL, connects the femur and tibia on the lateral side of the knee, on the outside surface. These ligaments prevent the bones from getting into an extreme bow-legged or knock-kneed arrangement. The classic clip block in American football can damage the MCL.

Within the knee joint are the two cruciate ligaments. Both begin on the tibia and insert within the large notch at the end of the femur. The anterior cruciate ligament (ACL) begins in the front and runs diagonally toward the lateral wall of the notch, while the larger posterior cruciate ligament (PCL) begins in the back and crosses behind the ACL to insert on the medial wall of the notch. These two ligaments prevent the femur and tibia from twisting on each other. The ACL also prevents the tibia from shifting too far forward, and the PCL prevents the tibia from shifting too far backward.

The knee also has a pair of crescent-shaped cups of cartilage called the medial meniscus and lateral meniscus. Another cartilage, called articular cartilage, covers the surfaces of the femur and tibia and the back of the patella. The two menisci and the articular cartilage support the free movement of the knee and are frequently damaged during sports such as soccer. An injury to the meniscus can create a sharp edge that can damage the articular cartilage, and when this happens, you are on the fast track to osteoarthritis. A big problem with an ACL injury and the resulting instability is the risk of early-onset arthritis.

The main actions of a hinge joint are flexion (bending the knee) and extension (extending the knee). But the knee is more than a hinge joint because of smaller but no less important movements such as rotation of the femur and tibia with each other. Another frequently mentioned movement is a valgus (knock-kneed) or varus (bow-legged) motion that usually occurs in response to some force exerted from the opposite side. A physician can test the varus and valgus instability of a knee by prying open the medial or lateral side of the joint, which sounds worse than it is. When you hear that someone tore an ACL when her knee went into an apparent valgus, the knee looks knock-kneed, but the actual motion is a combination of knee flexion and internal rotation of the femur at the hip. The knee is far more complex in its structure and function than we yet understand. Orthopedic surgeons who specialize in the knee learn something new nearly every day.

The fibula is a thin bone that runs parallel to the tibia. The bony connection between the tibia and fibula up near the knee is quite strong, but it is not as strong down at the ankle. Those large knots on the inside and outside of your ankle (each is called a malleolus) are actually the ends of each bone. They form a sort of pincer-like grasp on the top tarsal, the talus. Ligaments connect the ends of each bone with nearby tarsals to add stability to the ankle. The primary actions of the ankle are inversion and eversion plus plantar flexion and dorsiflexion. Inversion is rolling the sole of your foot inward, and eversion is rolling the sole outward. Flexion and extension of the foot are more properly called dorsiflexion (pointing your toes up) and plantar flexion (pointing your toes down). The powerful kicking motion is done with a plantar-flexed ankle. The anatomy of the ankle makes it likely that you will sprain the outside of your ankle (an inversion sprain) far more often than the inside of your ankle (an eversion sprain). With sufficient force, the talus can force the tibia and fibula out of parallel, resulting in what is often called a high ankle sprain.

Just like the hand and wrist, the ankle and foot have a dizzying array of ligaments for proper bony alignment. The same naming conventions for the bones of the hand and wrist apply, only with metatarsals instead of metacarpals.

Muscles of the Legs

Some of the muscles that originate on the pelvis, insert on the femur, and act to move the leg are described in chapter 6. The muscles that act on the knee, foot, and ankle are the topic of this chapter.

The thigh muscles are in three primary groups. The quadriceps femoris (the four-headed muscle in the thigh, or femoral, region) has four distinct originations. The three vasti muscles—the vastus medialis, vastus lateralis, and vastus intermedius—all begin along the long shaft of the femur (figure 8.1). (*Vastus* is Latin for *huge*.) The fourth head is the rectus femoris, which begins on the pelvis around the socket where the femur articulates with the pelvis. You can easily see three of the quads, but the vastus intermedius is underneath the other three. These four muscles come together to form the common quadriceps tendon that passes over the patella and down to insert on the knot on the tibia just beyond the knee. In one of those anatomical naming quirks, once the quadriceps tendon goes past the patella, its name changes to the patellar ligament. Since a muscle pulls its insertion toward its origin, when the quadriceps contracts, the knee extends. The rectus femoris begins on the pelvis and also assists in hip flexion.

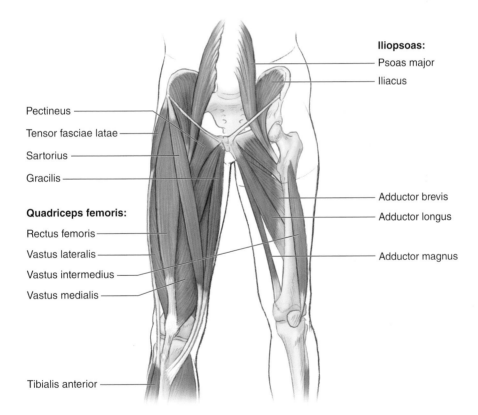

Figure 8.1   Muscles of the front of the leg.

The three muscles that make up the hamstrings (figure 8.2) are the opposite, antagonistic muscles to the quadriceps. They all begin on the pelvis. The biceps femoris is the lateral and largest of the three; it inserts down near the top of the fibula. The semitendinosus and semimembranosus run down the medial side of the thigh and insert behind the medial side of the knee. Most people can find at least two if not all three of these tendons. The main action of the hamstrings is knee flexion, but because all the muscles originate on the hip, they also perform hip extension. The hamstrings also play an important role in protecting the ACL from injury.

The muscles commonly referred to as the groin muscles all begin on the pelvis near the midline and run diagonally down and laterally to insert on the femur. Most are referred to as adductors, muscles that move the thigh toward the midline of the body. They range from quite small (pectineus) to progressively bigger (adductor brevis, adductor longus) to very large (adductor magnus) or very long (gracilis). The adductor longus is particularly susceptible to a strain injury in soccer players. All of these muscles assist in external rotation of the femur and more. You can't appreciate all these muscles do until you strain a groin and feel pain with nearly every step.

One final muscle of the thigh, sort of, is the tensor fasciae latae. The tensor fasciae latae is more tendon than muscle. This short, flat muscle originates on the crest of the hip, and the short fibers run down the outside of the thigh, ending roughly in the area of that knot felt on the side of your hip. Depending on your height, the fleshy portion might be 4 to 6 inches (10 to 15 cm) in length. From here, the tensor fasciae latae is mostly tendon all the way down the outside of the thigh, and it inserts on the mass of soft tissue that surrounds the knee. It abducts, medially (internally) rotates, and helps flex the hip.

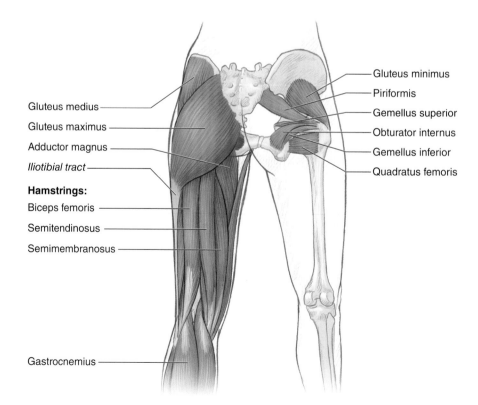

Figure 8.2 Muscles of the back of the leg.

Beyond the knee is a series of muscles that move the ankle, foot, and toes (figure 8.3). Originating along the front of the tibia are muscles that dorsiflex the ankle and others that go all the way to the toes for extension. On the lateral (outside) of the leg is a group of three peroneal muscles that originate on the fibula and mostly evert the foot but also assist in other actions. On the back of the leg are two major muscles. The gastrocnemius, which originates on the back of the femur and often is called the calf muscle, lies over the soleus, which originates on the tibia. The tendons of these two muscles join to become the Achilles tendon, which inserts on the heel (calcaneus). When these muscles contract, you rise up on your toes. They also contribute to your ability to jump and push off the ground during walking and running. These muscles are organized as distinct groups in the anterior, lateral, and posterior compartments of the leg. No muscles are considered medial.

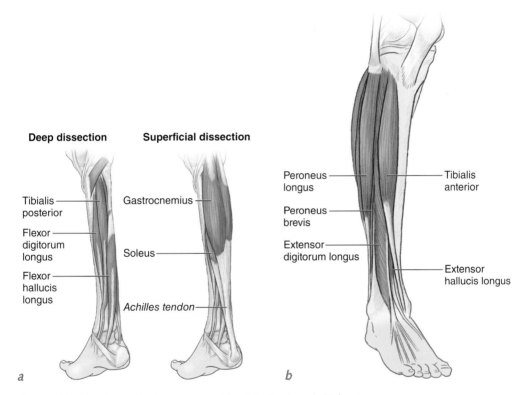

Figure 8.3 Muscles of the lower leg and foot: *(a)* back and *(b)* front.

Toe Raise Carrying Partner

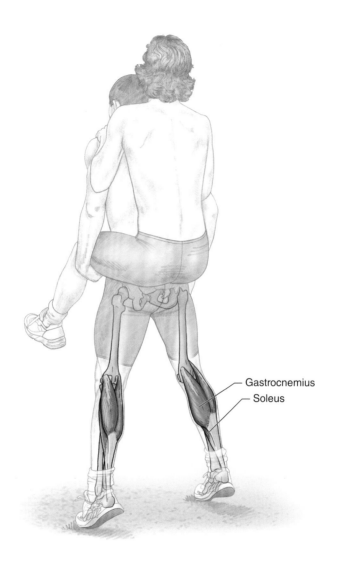

Gastrocnemius
Soleus

Execution

1. Find a partner who is about the same height and weight as you.
2. Have your partner climb onto your back in a piggyback fashion.
3. Perform slow, controlled toe raises by rising as high as possible with each attempt. Swap positions and repeat.

Muscles Involved

Primary: Gastrocnemius, soleus

Secondary: Erector spinae and other accessory back muscles (such as latissimus dorsi and external oblique)

Soccer Focus

Jumping power comes from the coordinated contribution of hip extension, knee extension, and plantar flexion (rising up on the toes). All these muscle groups need to be trained so that each can contribute appropriately during a jump. The calf muscles are also involved in running because much of the power in the push-off portion of the gait cycle comes from the gastrocnemius and soleus. This is especially true during the initial takeoff and acceleration in sprinting. The increase in stride length with faster speeds is in large part due to a stronger push-off from the gastrocnemius and the soleus. In addition, the calf muscles are strong contributors to the rigid locking of the ankle when striking the ball. Much of the power built up in the leg during the swing phase of kicking can be lost if the foot and ankle are not rigid at ball contact.

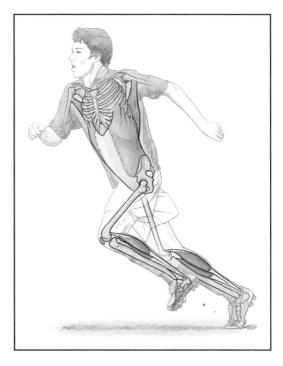

VARIATION

Machine Toe Raise

This exercise, also known as the standing calf raise, really isolates the gastrocnemius and soleus, with the gastrocnemius producing the more force of the two. The muscles can be further challenged by standing on a board or step to add an additional stretch over a greater range of motion. The demand on the soleus muscle increases if the knees are slightly bent during toe raises.

Partner Prone Leg Curl

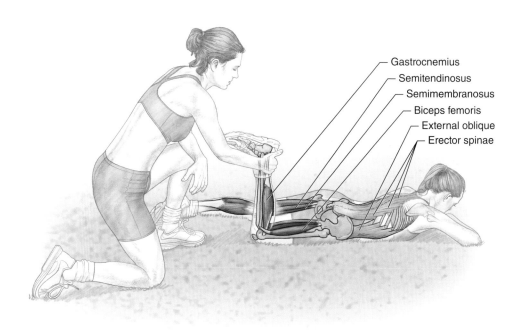

Gastrocnemius
Semitendinosus
Semimembranosus
Biceps femoris
External oblique
Erector spinae

Execution

1. Lie prone on the ground, with one knee extended and the other knee flexed.
2. Your partner kneels at your feet and holds the ankle of your flexed leg.
3. Perform knee flexion, curling the leg, while your partner resists the motion, allowing the flexion through the range of motion.
4. Switch legs and repeat with the other leg. After exercising both legs, switch places with your partner.

Muscles Involved

Primary: Hamstrings (biceps femoris, semitendinosus, semimembranosus), gastrocnemius

Secondary: Abdominal core (external oblique, internal oblique, transversus abdominis, rectus abdominis), erector spinae for core stabilization and posture

Soccer Focus

For earlier generations of soccer players, a hamstring strain was a rare injury. The pace and ballistic nature of the modern game have made this previously rare injury the number one soccer injury, according to some studies. Some studies show that professional teams see six or more hamstring strains a year. And these take awhile to heal, which means a team could be without a number of core players for an extended period of time. There are three risk factors for a hamstring strain. The strongest predictor of a strain, or almost any injury, is a history of a previous strain injury. Next, the older the player, the more likely he is to suffer a strain. Finally, poor hamstring strength increases the risk of a strain. Notice that of these three factors, the only one that can be modified is strength. Thus, it is wise to improve hamstring strength to prevent this serious strain injury.

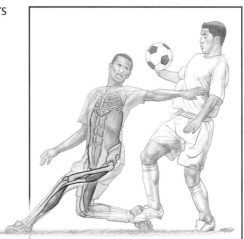

VARIATION

Machine Knee Flexion

Hamstring strength can be improved by using a machine designed for standing, prone, or seated leg curls. Regardless of the positioning, the knee flexion isolates the motion to the hamstrings and will effectively increase strength. The greatest strength gain and reduction in strain injury come from performing the hamstrings exercise, sometimes called the Nordic curl, in the FIFA warm-up (page 30).

Lying Adduction

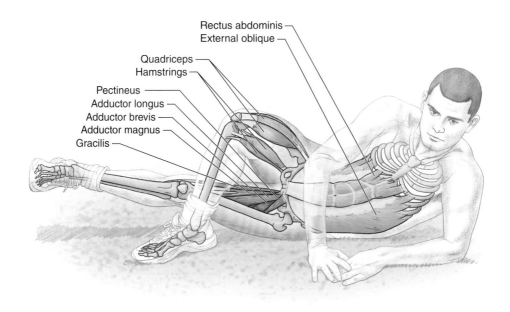

Rectus abdominis
External oblique
Quadriceps
Hamstrings
Pectineus
Adductor longus
Adductor brevis
Adductor magnus
Gracilis

Execution

1. Lie on the ground on your side.
2. Flex your upper leg, and place the foot flat on the ground in front of the thigh of the lower leg. The lower leg is fully extended.
3. Slowly raise the lower leg off the ground. Hold briefly at the highest position, and then return to the starting position.
4. Switch sides and repeat on the other leg.

Muscles Involved

Primary: Adductors (adductor longus, adductor brevis, adductor magnus, pectineus, gracilis)

Secondary: Abdominal core for posture, quadriceps (vastus medialis, vastus lateralis, vastus intermedius, rectus femoris) and hamstrings to maintain an extended knee

Soccer Focus

A sport's pattern of activity can lead to some particular deficiencies. Soccer players are famous for poor flexibility about the knee, groin, and ankle. Are these weaknesses due to the nature of the sport or the lack of attention to improving flexibility? Poor flexibility is considered a risk factor for a variety of injuries including groin strains, which can happen while defending or blocking a pass or shot; while taking a very hard shot; or during a rapid reactive change of direction. The most commonly injured groin muscle is the adductor longus. Most people don't realize how much the groin muscles are used during normal daily activities until one is injured. The leg is attached to the pelvis through a ball-and-socket joint (the hip) that allows the leg to pivot around the joint. During flexion and extension, the leg can move through a rather large cone-shaped range of motion, but the action of the adductors helps minimize the sideways motion of the leg as it moves through hip flexion and extension. Those who have suffered groin strains usually are receptive to supplemental exercises that help strengthen the adductors to prevent or delay the next strain. Another pesky groin injury is a sports hernia, sometimes called athletic pubalgia (see chapter 2, page 16). Although the pain is situated in the groin, the actual problem can lie elsewhere, and the player may not be able to recall exactly when the injury occurred. See a sports medicine physician for an accurate diagnosis because the treatments for a groin strain and a sports hernia are quite different.

VARIATION

Cable Hip Adduction

The lying adduction exercise can be performed on the field. But the only way to continue to train the adductors on the field is to do more repetitions, increasing local muscle endurance more than pure strength of the adductors. (I have even seen some teams bring ankle weights to the field.) To really increase adductor strength, go to the weight room and use the cable machine so you can add resistance.

Fire Hydrant

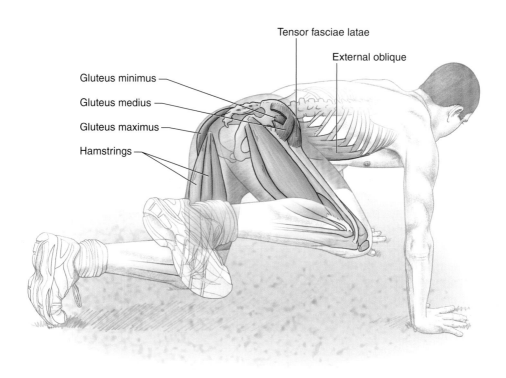

Tensor fasciae latae

External oblique

Gluteus minimus

Gluteus medius

Gluteus maximus

Hamstrings

Execution

1. Get on all fours on the ground.
2. Raise one flexed leg to the side until the leg is parallel to the ground. Pause briefly and then lower the leg back to the starting position.
3. Switch legs, raising the other leg to the side until it is parallel to the ground. Alternate legs.

Muscles Involved

Primary: Gluteals (gluteus maximus, medius, and minimus), tensor fasciae latae

Secondary: Vastus lateralis, hamstrings, abdominal core for posture and balance

Soccer Focus

The hip is a curious joint when it comes to sports injury. Not many players remember a specific inciting event, one they can pinpoint as causing the hip injury. But a substantial number of retired players have undergone total hip replacements at an age most would consider too young for new hips. It seems the lack of control of the femur within the pelvis causes minor defects in the socket portion of the joint that, over time, will wear down and eventually need to be replaced. Because strength is important in joint stability, look for exercises such as this one that can be used to improve the muscles around the hip joint. This exercise works the various muscles involved in hip abduction. At the same time, when done properly by taking the thigh through a wide range of motion, the fire hydrant is also a great dynamic stretch of the adductors. It should be easy to see where this exercise gets its name.

VARIATION

Machine Abduction

Most activities have both a field and a machine-based version. This machine exercise is done in a seated posture. Place your knees between the padded arms of the machine, and spread your legs as much as possible. Varying the angle of the seat is said to change the primary location of the muscle fibers being recruited.

Cable Kickback

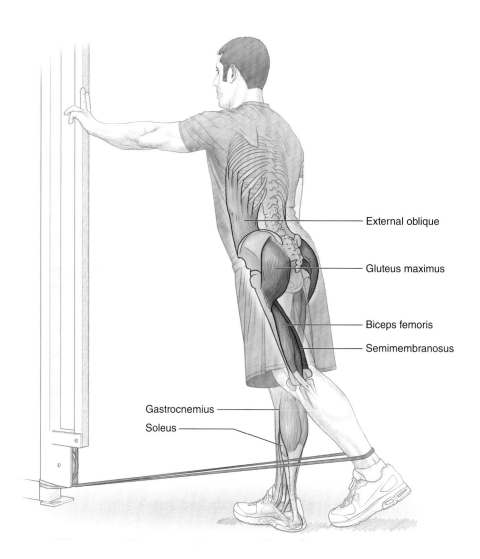

External oblique

Gluteus maximus

Biceps femoris

Semimembranosus

Gastrocnemius

Soleus

Execution

1. Stand and face a cable machine or other stable object. Loop the rope or strap or a resistance band around one ankle.

2. Keeping the leg as straight as possible, extend the leg at the hip (move it backward) as far as possible. Pause briefly and then return to the starting position. If necessary, hold onto the machine for balance.

3. Switch legs and repeat with the other leg.

Muscles Involved

Primary: Gluteus maximus, hamstrings

Secondary: Abdominal core for posture, muscles of the balancing leg (such as quadriceps, gastrocnemius, soleus, peroneus longus, peroneus brevis, and peroneus tertius)

Soccer Focus

Any movement that results in a ball being thrown or kicked requires some sort of a windup. The longer the windup, the farther or faster the ball will go. The anatomy of the hip joint as well as a specific ligament of the hip (the iliofemoral, or Y ligament) limits the backswing of a kick. Kicking is not just about the forward swing of the kicking leg. You can increase your power by increasing the strength of the hip extensors so that you use as much of the motion available for the windup as possible.

Seated Leg Extension

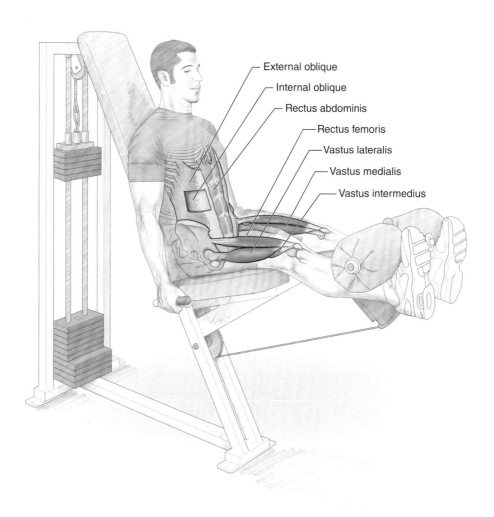

External oblique

Internal oblique

Rectus abdominis

Rectus femoris

Vastus lateralis

Vastus medialis

Vastus intermedius

Execution

1. Adjust the seat height of the leg extension machine as needed and take a seat. Hook your ankles underneath the pads.
2. Extend the knees. Pause at the top of the movement, and then slowly return to the starting position. Repeat.

Muscles Involved

Primary: Quadriceps

Secondary: Abdominal core for seated posture

Soccer Focus

Knee extension is one of the more obvious movements of kicking. Once the backswing ceases, the hip flexes while the knee remains flexed. As the knee gets close to the ball, hip extension slows and knee extension accelerates rapidly until ball contact. (Actually, the leg starts to slow just before ball contact.) The rapid acceleration of knee extension is what imparts a large fraction of the power for a shot or a long pass. Many studies have attempted to show what weight training does for kicking ability and, while it helps, it's not as much as you might think. If you want to kick the ball harder or farther, you will gain the most by kicking and a little from lifting. Be realistic about the goals of strength training. For the knee, strength training is about increasing strength to prevent injury, not necessarily to improve kicking performance.

VARIATION

Single-Leg Extension

This exercise can be done with one leg at a time. For some athletes, the stronger leg will do the bulk of the work during a bilateral exercise, and the weaker leg will go along for the ride. The single-leg extension works one leg at a time, ensuring both legs receive the optimal training stimulus. Also, this and other lifts can be modified by taking twice the time to lower the weight as it takes to raise the weight.

Stability Ball Leg Curl

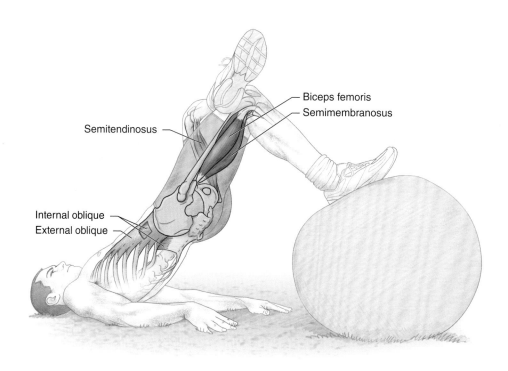

Biceps femoris

Semimembranosus

Semitendinosus

Internal oblique

External oblique

Execution

1. Lie on the ground, and place the heel of one foot high up on the stability ball. Cross the other leg over the knee. Raise your trunk off the ground, and put the weight on your shoulders.

2. Flex the knee, and roll the ball from under the heel to the sole of the foot as far as possible. Pause and then slowly return to the starting position. Switch legs and repeat.

Muscles Involved

Primary: Hamstrings

Secondary: Abdominal core for balance

Soccer Focus

The Soccer Focus section for the partner prone leg curl (page 155) covers the importance of strengthening the hamstrings to protect them from a muscle strain injury. The hamstrings also figure into anterior cruciate ligament tears. Remember, the ACL begins on the front portion of the flat surface of the tibia (leg bone) and courses back to the lateral surface within a big notch at the end of the femur (thigh bone), so it goes in sort of a diagonal direction. Think about its configuration. If you twist your right tibia in a clockwise direction, the ligament gets looser, but if you twist the right tibia in a counterclockwise direction, the ligament tightens. That's not all. If the tibia slides backward under the femur, the ligament loosens, but if the tibia slides forward, the ligament tightens. The tibia slides forward every time you land from a jump or plant a foot to make a cut. Imagine if the hamstrings contracted just as the tibia started to slide forward. What would happen? The tibia wouldn't slide forward as far, and you would have protected the ACL from being stretched through the contraction of the strong hamstrings and by calling on the hamstrings at the right time after learning how to land and cut. Strong hamstrings are very important in team sports such as soccer.

Many of the exercises in this book are isolation exercises. They are designed to isolate movement to specific muscles or muscle groups. These exercises are very effective at ensuring those specific muscles and their actions get the full benefit of training.

In sports, however, actions are rarely isolated. In a game, dynamic planned and reactive movements involve multiple joints and muscles in a coordinated pattern to achieve something as simple as bending over to place the ball to take a corner kick or as highly complex as a plant, cut, and turn with one touch of the ball. It is quite impossible to mimic every action of a sport with a supplemental exercise or even with what some call functional exercises. You would spend more time on those than on the actual sport itself.

The exercises in this chapter provide a glimpse into what is possible for more complex multijoint activities. Although few of these exercises mimic any particular sport, each requires components common to most sports, including soccer. Because the power output of soccer is driven by the lower extremities, these exercises are all about improving leg power for running, cutting, stopping, jumping, maintaining static and reactive balance, and more.

It is important to include complex supplemental actions in physical training. You plan to plant your right foot and cut to the left, but your studs don't dig in as expected, or dig in too much, and you react with a slight skip or hop and adjust your posture to keep your balance during this seemingly minor adjustment. Most of the actions and reactions are handled by the cerebellum and spinal cord. If all your supplemental training activities were simple single-joint, single-muscle-group actions, your body would miss a valuable opportunity to train adaptations to support skilled performance. This is why you hear a lot about functional training.

A common adage, if a little simplistic, is the so-called 10-year and 10,000-hour rule, which says that the truly elite achieved that elite status after putting in about 10 years and 10,000 hours of deliberate practice in their chosen fields. Although a great deal of the learning involved over the years is tactical, much of neuromuscular learning is the ability to use only those muscle cells necessary to perform a skill. Think of children learning to bounce a ball. They use their entire bodies—trunk, hips, legs, shoulders, and arms. Everything parallels the up and down movement of the ball. As they improve, they learn to rule out unnecessary muscle cells, eventually using the bare minimum. Watch professionals play, and you will see a midfielder on the run place a pass right in the stride of a running teammate. The passer had to gauge her own speed and the speed of her teammate, decide how to pass the ball (with or without spin, on the ground, in the air, with what part of the foot), and determine how hard to hit the ball (not so hard that it outpaces the receiver and not so soft that the receiver runs past the ball). I guarantee that not one of those decisions was done consciously. All had been pushed to the subconscious and used only the muscle cells necessary to make a difficult pass look simple. One part of that 10-year, 10,000-hour rule is that motor skills become mostly rote and unconscious so the conscious brain can focus on planning, predicting, reacting, adjusting, and anything else that might fall under the executive function heading of *tactics*. All our midfielder did consciously was choose whom to pass to, a tactical decision. The rest was automatic.

Back-to-Back Squat

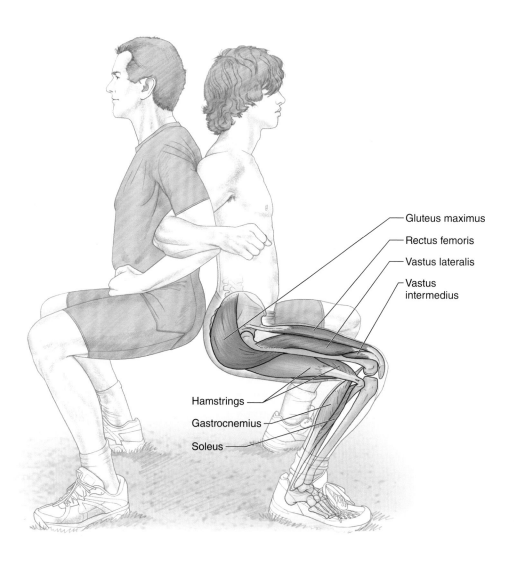

Gluteus maximus

Rectus femoris

Vastus lateralis

Vastus intermedius

Hamstrings

Gastrocnemius

Soleus

Execution

1. You will need a partner of similar height and weight for this exercise. Stand back to back with your partner, feet about shoulder-width apart.

2. Hook elbows with your partner, and lean back into each other as if leaning against a wall. There should be about 2 feet (.6 m) between your heels and your partner's heels.

3. In unison, squat down until your knees form 90-degree angles. Return to a standing position.

Muscles Involved

Primary: Quadriceps (vastus medialis, vastus lateralis, vastus intermedius, rectus femoris), gluteus maximus

Secondary: Hamstrings (biceps femoris, semitendinosus, semimembranosus), adductors (adductor longus, adductor brevis, adductor magnus, pectineus, gracilis), erector spinae, gastrocnemius, soleus

Soccer Focus

Soccer requires explosive movements at a moment's notice: the goalkeeper pushing hard against the ground to dive across the face of the goal and make a save, the defender jumping high to clear a cross, or the striker leaping to head a shot. All of these require high power output from the hip extensors, knee extensors, and ankle plantar flexors. A coordinated pattern of movement from strong muscles is needed for maximum jump height and distance. All players would be wise to perform squats like these because the increased strength and power will be used frequently in a match. Although each muscle group can be trained separately, a compound movement such as a squat better simulates conditions faced in competition.

VARIATION

Racked Squat

Use a barbell and perform traditional squats within a safety rack. The rack supports the bar. Step under the bar, position it appropriately in the correct posture, and then stand up. The safety supports are removed, and the exercise begins. Safety stops are positioned a little below the level of the shoulders when the knees are bent to about 90 degrees.

Partner Carry Squat

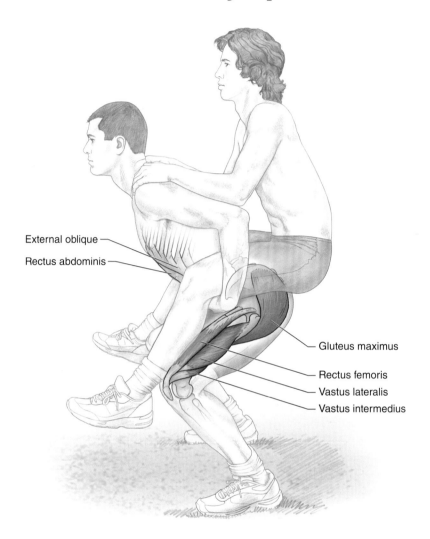

External oblique

Rectus abdominis

Gluteus maximus

Rectus femoris

Vastus lateralis

Vastus intermedius

Execution

1. As in toe raise carrying partner (chapter 8, page 152), choose a partner of equal height and weight. Be careful when choosing a partner because this exercise can be demanding on the knees. This exercise isn't just about up-and-down strength; it is also about balance. Have your partner climb on your back in a traditional piggyback position.

2. With your legs comfortably apart and your partner centered on your back (you'll probably be leaning forward a little), perform a partial squat to about a 45-degree angle at the knees. Do not squat beyond 90 degrees of knee flexion.

3. Squat slowly. Pause briefly at the bottom of the squat before returning to the starting position and repeating. After finishing your repetitions, switch places with your partner.

Muscles Involved

Primary: Quadriceps, gluteus maximus

Secondary: Adductors, erector spinae and abdominal core (external oblique, internal oblique, transversus abdominis, rectus abdominis) for posture

Soccer Focus

The traditional squat exercise has numerous variations. One reason squat exercises are often included in any supplemental training program for sport is that they activate multiple muscles and several joints to perform the movement and maintain balance. The primary muscle groups for the movement are the quadriceps femoris for knee extension and the gluteus maximus for hip extension. One of the most important aspects of performing any squat is posture. Correct posture activates the abdominal core and erector spinae muscles during the squat. Widening the stance increases the involvement of the adductors. Never discount the importance of the force produced by these muscles during close physical contact during play. The player with the stronger hips, back, core, and quads will be at a distinct advantage during tackling and other player-to-player challenges.

VARIATION

Hack Squat

The hack squat is a good way to work the quads and glutes without having to carry the weight on your shoulders. It is also a good choice for those who are not well skilled at a traditional squat. When placing yourself in the machine, make sure your knees and toes point in the same direction. The general thought is that the higher you place your feet on the platform, the more you use your glutes; the lower your feet are on the platform, the more you use your quads. Get advice on technique before attempting this exercise.

Split-Leg Squat

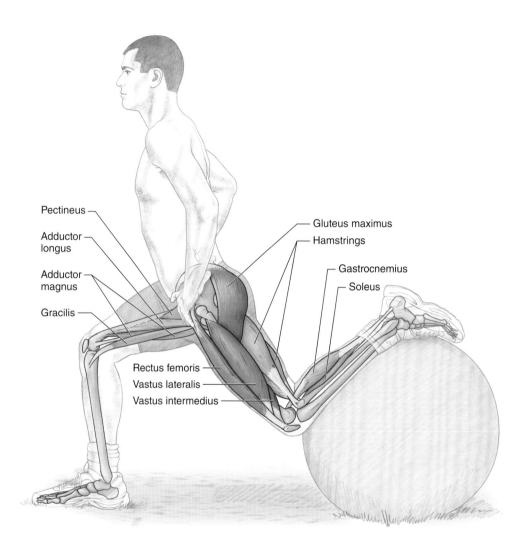

Pectineus

Adductor longus

Adductor magnus

Gracilis

Rectus femoris

Vastus lateralis

Vastus intermedius

Gluteus maximus

Hamstrings

Gastrocnemius

Soleus

Execution

1. Stand on one leg. Reach back with the other leg, placing the ankle or shin on top of a stability ball.
2. Flex the forward knee to about a 90-degree angle while rolling the ball backward with the trailing leg.
3. Return to the starting position.

Muscles Involved

Primary: Quadriceps, gluteus maximus

Secondary: Hamstrings, adductors, erector spinae, gastrocnemius, soleus

Soccer Focus

Flex the forward knee, and roll the ball back a bit to prevent your forward knee from going beyond your foot. Motor control of the knee is emphasized repeatedly in soccer, and this exercise is a good test of your ability to control your knee during a functional movement. The knee should not waver to the right or left, nor should it completely cover the foot. The strength and balance required by an exercise such as this should help control the lower body during the ballistic and reactive actions of cutting and landing from jumps, adding even more protection to the knee. Use a spotter or support if needed when assuming the starting position. Good balance and quad strength are needed for this exercise, so if either is lacking, this might not be the best initial option until you have improved both. Carrying dumbbells in each hand or an unloaded barbell on the shoulders, adding weight as strength improves, can make this exercise even harder.

Low Hurdle

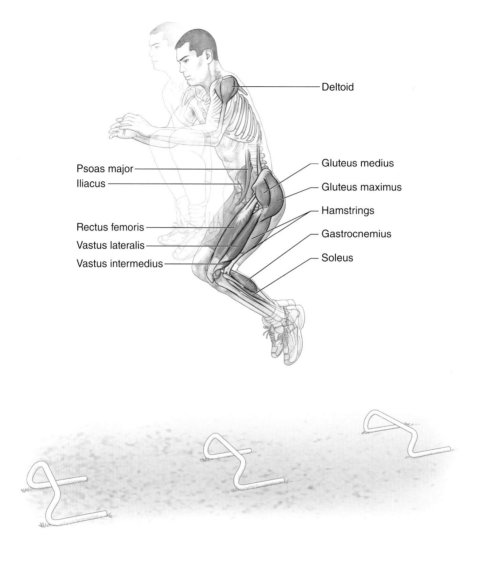

Deltoid

Psoas major
Iliacus

Rectus femoris
Vastus lateralis
Vastus intermedius

Gluteus medius
Gluteus maximus
Hamstrings
Gastrocnemius
Soleus

Execution

1. Set up a series of hurdles in a straight line, 3 to 5 feet (about 1 to 1.5 m) apart.

2. Approach the first hurdle with a step or two, and jump over the hurdle. Use a two-foot takeoff and landing. You will need to tuck your legs up to your chest to clear each hurdle.

3. Jump the subsequent hurdles with as little time on the ground as possible between hurdles. Think of this more as a series of rebounds than separate jumps.

Muscles Involved

Primary: Gluteus maximus, gluteus medius, quadriceps, gastrocnemius, soleus

Secondary: Hip flexors (rectus femoris, psoas major and minor, iliacus, sartorius), erector spinae, deltoid, hamstrings

Soccer Focus

Repeated jumping is a common training task across generations of soccer players, and it benefits players in many ways. For example, each takeoff helps improve leg strength for jumping. Each landing teaches the player how to land safely if the coach is watching and offering advice on landing form. Functional and reactive balance is required throughout the task. An understanding of the length of the legs and the force needed to just clear each hurdle keeps the player from falling or working too hard. The plyometric aspect makes this task one of the best functional exercises for improving jumping ability. (Plyometric exercises apply a stretch right before the muscle contracts. This makes the subsequent jump higher. If you squat and hold the position and then jump, you will not jump as high as if you squatted and immediately jumped with no pause. The pause negates the effect of the stretch during the squat.) This exercise features reciprocal jumps over hurdles, but the same concept can be used with a speed ladder or back and forth or side to side movements across a line. Some coaches still ask players to jump over a ball, but this is not advised because landing on the ball can cause any number of injuries.

Step-Up

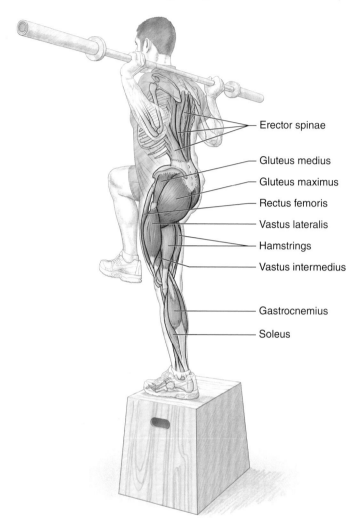

Erector spinae

Gluteus medius

Gluteus maximus

Rectus femoris

Vastus lateralis

Hamstrings

Vastus intermedius

Gastrocnemius

Soleus

Execution

1. Stand in front of a bench or box that is between shin and knee height. Using an overhand grip, hold an unweighted bar on your shoulders.

2. With the lead leg, step up onto the bench or box. Continue the step-up until the lead leg is straight, but keep raising the trail leg, knee flexed, until the thigh is parallel to the ground. The trail leg does not touch the bench or box.

3. Step back down, leading with the trail leg.

4. Switch legs and repeat, leading with the opposite leg.

Muscles Involved

Primary: Quadriceps, gluteus maximus, gluteus medius

Secondary: Erector spinae, hamstrings, gastrocnemius, soleus, adductors

Soccer Focus

We all know that the dominant hand is the one we write with. But which is your dominant leg? Is it the leg you use for your hardest goal kick or the leg you use to take off for a long jump? Most of us have a dominant leg that works more than the nondominant leg when both legs are active at the same time. Single-leg exercises have some advantages over exercises that work both legs simultaneously. When the legs work one at a time to provide all the force, each leg gets worked equally without one picking up the slack for the other, although the entire exercise does take a little longer. And the benefits are not just for strength. Each leg is required to apply motor control of the knee and whole-body balance, two important factors for preventing injury, especially to the knee. Pay close attention to posture for safety as well as core stability.

Forward Lunge

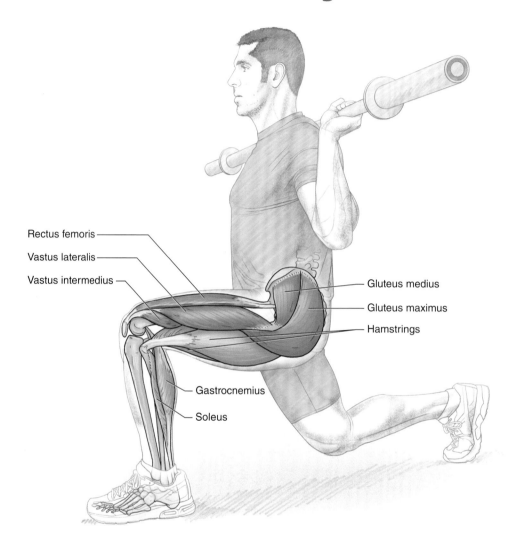

Rectus femoris

Vastus lateralis

Vastus intermedius

Gluteus medius

Gluteus maximus

Hamstrings

Gastrocnemius

Soleus

Execution

1. Hold a barbell in an overhand grip. Stand and place the barbell on your shoulders.

2. Step forward far enough so that when the lunge is complete, your leading knee is at a 90-degree angle and that thigh is parallel to the floor. The trailing knee will likely be just above the floor.

3. Step back to return to the starting position. Repeat with the opposite leg. Alternate legs on each lunge.

Muscles Involved

Primary: Gluteus maximus, gluteus medius, quadriceps

Secondary: Erector spinae, hamstrings, gastrocnemius, soleus, adductors

Soccer Focus

This exercise differs slightly from the lunge in chapter 2, which is used for dynamic flexibility of the hip and groin. In this version, you stay in one place and use a bar. This variation is more of a strength exercise and is highly valued by conditioning experts who create programs for the eccentric, concentric, and balance requirements of a number of different sports. Keep the back straight, and keep the head up and looking forward. At the end of the lunge, do not allow the leading knee to go beyond the toes or wobble across the long axis of the foot. Poor strength or fatigue can affect proper execution. If you struggle to perform the lunge correctly, reduce the load being carried, shorten the length of the lunge, or allow more recovery time between lunges to prevent fatigue.

VARIATION

Side Lunge

Being able to control the knee during a change of direction is an important feature of knee injury prevention. When doing a side lunge, the knee of the leading leg must be over the supporting foot and not wobbling back and forth.

Goalies

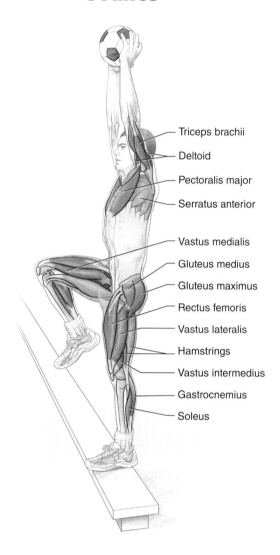

Triceps brachii
Deltoid
Pectoralis major
Serratus anterior
Vastus medialis
Gluteus medius
Gluteus maximus
Rectus femoris
Vastus lateralis
Hamstrings
Vastus intermedius
Gastrocnemius
Soleus

Execution

1. Stand in front of a low bench. Hold a soccer ball in both hands.

2. In a smooth motion, step up onto the bench with your lead leg, continuing the step-up until the knee of the lead leg is fully extended. Swing the trailing flexed knee as high as possible as you fully extend both arms overhead.

3. Reverse this smooth movement to return to the starting position.

4. Switch legs and repeat, leading with the opposite leg. Alternate legs with each repetition.

Muscles Involved

Primary: Quadriceps, gluteals (gluteus maximus, medius, and minimus), gastrocnemius, soleus, deltoid, triceps brachii, pectoralis major

Secondary: Hamstrings, erector spinae, trapezius, serratus anterior

Soccer Focus

As the name suggests, this exercise is great for goalkeepers, but it also is useful for all players. Think about all the key movements needed to run and jump for a ball in the air. The main difference between a field player and a goalkeeper is that the goalie gets to reach up with the arms and hands. Both the field player and the goalkeeper must approach the area, plan the timing, decide which is the best takeoff leg, gather for the jump, extend and push off to leave the ground to contact the ball at the top of the jump, and then safely land. The emphasis of this exercise includes everything up to the takeoff and is an efficient way to apply the various individual lower-extremity exercises into one functional task.

VARIATION

Stadium Stair Goalies

A reasonable alternative uses stadium or bleacher steps, and you carry dumbbells instead of a ball. Take every other step, pressing the dumbbell in the hand opposite the stepping leg. You may choose to raise both arms on each step.

Rebound Jump

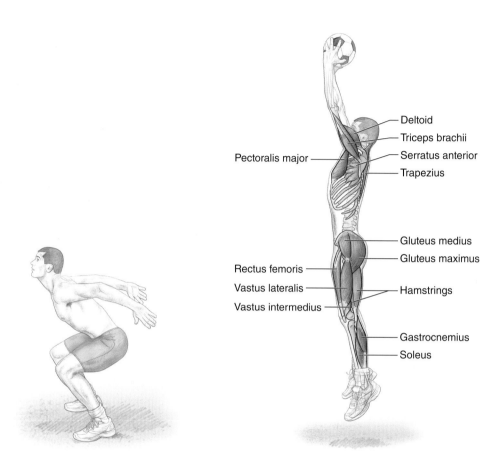

Deltoid

Triceps brachii

Serratus anterior

Trapezius

Pectoralis major

Gluteus medius

Gluteus maximus

Rectus femoris

Vastus lateralis

Vastus intermedius

Hamstrings

Gastrocnemius

Soleus

Execution

1. You will need a partner for this exercise. Face your partner. Your partner is holding a soccer ball.
2. Your partner forcefully bounces the ball on the ground. Using a two-leg takeoff, jump and catch the ball at the top of your jump.
3. Make sure you stick the landing. Do not let your knees wobble back and forth over your feet when you contact the ground.
4. To avoid fatigue from frequent maximal jumps, it is best for you and your partner to alternate jumps.

Muscles Involved

Primary: Quadriceps, gluteals, gastrocnemius, soleus, deltoid, triceps brachii, pectoralis major

Secondary: Hamstrings, erector spinae, trapezius, serratus anterior

Soccer Focus

The rebound jump exercise might be considered a functional extension of the goalies exercise (page 180), which did not require you to actually leave the ground. The rebound jump exercise requires significant timing because so much has to happen in order for you to get to the takeoff point, jump, and catch the ball at the peak of your jump, as a goalie might do during a match. This usually requires some movement on the jumper's part (the bounce rarely goes straight up) and correct timing to coordinate the ball's descent and your takeoff so you can catch the ball as high as possible. But it doesn't end there because you have to land safely. Many of the exercises in this book require that the knees flex and be over the feet when landing so that the knees do not wobble back and forth. Although all your attention is on the jump and catch, you can't forget about the landing. Try to land quietly, absorbing the shock of impact. Most players like the challenges—the bounce, the jump, and the landing—of this exercise.

VARIATION

Single-Leg Rebound Jump

A simple variation is to use a single-leg takeoff. In most instances, the two-leg rebound jump is done when the ball is bounced nearly straight up. For this variation, the ball should be thrown to the ground in such a way that you have to run a little and jump for the ball from a single-leg takeoff, landing on both feet.

Lying Machine Squat

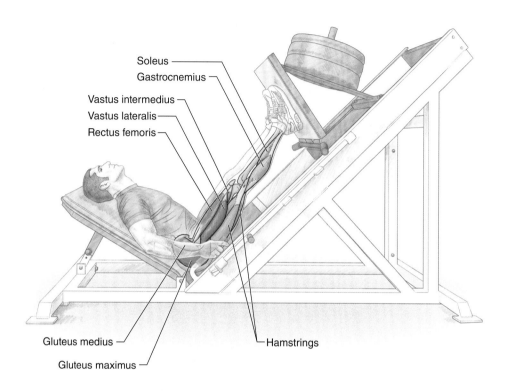

Soleus
Gastrocnemius
Vastus intermedius
Vastus lateralis
Rectus femoris
Gluteus medius
Gluteus maximus
Hamstrings

Execution

1. Adjust the machine so that when you get in, your knees are bent a little less than 90 degrees and your feet are about shoulder-width apart. You may prefer to point the feet out slightly.

2. Position your feet on the platform so that your knees do not obscure your feet. Rest your back and head on the sled, with your shoulders pressed into the shoulder pads. Grasp the handles.

3. As you exhale, press against the platform through the balls of your feet, and move the sled until your hips and knees are extended.

4. After a brief pause, inhale and slowly return to a knee angle of 90 degrees. This is not as far a movement as the initial starting movement.

5. After the last repetition, slowly return the sled back to the starting position.

Muscles Involved

Primary: Quadriceps, gluteus maximus, gluteus medius

Secondary: Gastrocnemius, soleus, adductors, hamstrings

Soccer Focus

The value of the squat cannot be overstated. It works multiple muscles and joints over a wide range of motion while requiring posture and balance—a big strength bang for the training buck. The modern game is more congested than ever as bigger and faster players compete on the same size field using defensive tactics designed to make the field even more compact. Contact is inevitable, and the stronger player will be better prepared to withstand the contact and either gain or maintain control of the ball. No one wants to see the individual brilliance of a player stifled and smothered by big, strong players. Neither does anyone want to see that brilliant player put out of play because of an injury. While nothing says that a smaller player will always be more skillful and entertaining or that a bigger, stronger player can't be as skillful, both players need to be well prepared for the unavoidable contact that is common at higher levels of play.

Woodchopper

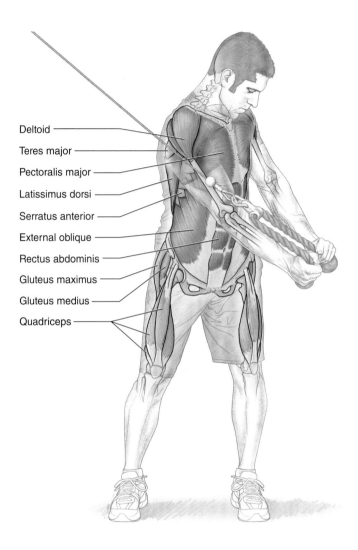

Deltoid

Teres major

Pectoralis major

Latissimus dorsi

Serratus anterior

External oblique

Rectus abdominis

Gluteus maximus

Gluteus medius

Quadriceps

Execution

1. Stand sideways to and a slight distance from a high pulley. Lift your arms to grasp the rope, strap, or handle with both hands.

2. Start by pulling the rope down and across your body. As your hands pass your shoulders, twist the trunk and crunch your abs. Flex your knees slightly as you continue this diagonal pull toward the opposite knee.

3. Slowly and under control, reverse the movement to return to the starting position. After completing the desired number of repetitions, turn around and repeat the exercise in the opposite direction.

Muscles Involved

Primary: Rectus abdominis, external oblique, internal oblique, deltoid, latissimus dorsi, pectoralis major

Secondary: Quadriceps, gluteals, teres major, serratus anterior

Soccer Focus

This whole-body exercise has many benefits. The action recruits the arms, trunk, gluteals, and quads in a stepwise, coordinated movement. There are no shortcuts, as one action must precede the next. On the surface, the arms and abs seem to be the focus, but the legs also play an important role as the base around which the actions occur. Pay attention to the position of the knees over the feet, and don't let the knees wobble back and forth. This is a very good functional exercise that involves multiple muscles and actions. Multijoint activities such as this are very useful supplemental exercises for the whole-body demands of team sports such as soccer. Some instructions do not include trunk flexion and the squat, making it an arm extension and trunk rotation exercise.

WHOLE-BODY TRAINING FOR SOCCER

Throughout this book, the strength training focus has been on isolating a movement and the muscles involved in that movement. The strength training shelf of any commercial bookstore or library will display dozens of books that show how to train muscles in isolation. This concept ensures that every muscle is fully activated and will adapt to the new imposed demand.

The next step is to incorporate the muscles to function as part of a whole system, sort of the athlete's version of the whole being greater than the sum of its parts. Athletic performance is not done in isolation. Rather, the whole of performance is greater than the result of the sum of the neuromuscular parts. Performance in sport is a combination of the technique required for that sport, the specific fitness (physical and psychological) for that sport, and the unique tactics for success. Some of these are planned and some are reactions to the opposition, but all evolve over time as advances force the sport to change. Any opportunity to involve multiple parts of the whole system will move the player closer to being able to execute the coach's vision of the sport. This is especially crucial in team sports since the outcome is influenced by so many things—each individual player, the interactions of small and large group play, the style of play, the style of the opposition, the referee, the environment, the crowd, and more.

The options presented in this chapter have one common thread: They all require multiple joints, muscles, and muscle actions. No exercise is done in isolation. Coaches who have experience with or exposure to earlier training methods might recognize that similar field-based exercises formed the core of fitness circuits found in coaching books dating back to the 1960s and earlier.

Although players from the old country might remember similar exercises in their training programs, those programs were deficient in the basic training fundamentals: frequency, intensity, duration, and progression. They might have done comparable exercises but can't recall doing things as frequently or as intensely or for as long as what is currently in vogue. And their training certainly was not periodized over a long competitive calendar. What is seen today is a reincorporation of earlier modes of training into modern training principles.

The goal of these and other whole-body activities is to prepare players for the strategic actions that will lead to success either in scoring or preventing goals. Those actions frequently require high power output for jumping or sprinting. Repetitive jumping is a plyometric activity, and various versions are used to take advantage of the stretch–shortening cycle that is known to improve power output not just in jumping but also in sprinting. If improvement in sprinting is a goal (and it should be), look at what track sprinters are doing and you will see plenty of exercises directed toward repetitive jumping.

Incorporating whole-body training tools helps in coordinating the body during the random actions that occur every few seconds in a soccer game. Players will jump, hop, skip, leap, and cut at a moment's notice, often without any conscious thought at the time to the action or reaction. Although it is difficult to plan training to mimic what actually happens when facing a real opponent (as opposed to a teammate in training), it is not difficult to prepare each player's neuromuscular system to be ready to make sudden reactions to unforeseen circumstances during a match. And it's the responsibility of the coach to make sure each player is as prepared as possible. This is why it's more the norm today to see players doing guided activities that on the surface appear unrelated to the game. These might involve benches, hoops, hurdles, speed ladders, and other tools of the trade that will teach players to use their bodies efficiently with as few unnecessary movements as possible. Although the running form of a soccer player will rarely be mistaken for the smooth and efficient form of a sprinter, a comparison of soccer video clips from a few decades ago to today's game should be proof enough that the training, coordination, and athleticism have advanced considerably.

Despite all the training advances of the past 25 years, none of them will produce the desired benefit if coaches and players fail to heed the lessons of experts in other supplementary aspects of performance. Consider the following:

• Research has shown that as little as 2 percent dehydration can lead to impaired performance. Don't use the running clock in soccer as an excuse not to drink during a match. There are plenty of dead-ball opportunities to take a drink. On really hot days, the ref has the authority to stop play for a fluid break. A water break is part of the rules in numerous youth leagues during hot and humid conditions. Did you notice the water break in each half of the men's gold medal game at the Beijing Olympics?

• It has been reported that between 25 and 40 percent of soccer players are dehydrated before they even step on the field for training or competition because they have failed to adequately rehydrate after the previous day's training or competition.

• Muscle requires fuel, and the primary fuel for a sport such as soccer is carbohydrate. Restricting carbohydrate will only hinder performance. Players who enter the game with a less than optimal tank of fuel will walk more and run less, especially late in the match when most goals are scored. For some reason, team sport athletes are not as conscientious about their food selections as individual sport athletes are.

• Injuries increase with time in each half, suggesting a fitness component to injury prevention. One aspect of injury prevention is to improve each player's fitness. Players should arrive at camp with a reasonable fitness level so that the coach can safely raise the fitness of the players even further through directed preseason training. Many teams have a very dense competition schedule, making it hard to raise fitness further during the season. Those who try to improve fitness each week with too much high-intensity work during a match-dense season risk acute and overuse injury, poor performance, slow recovery, and the possibility of overtraining.

• Some reports suggest that less skilled players suffer more injuries than do more highly skilled players. Thus, another way to prevent injuries is to improve skill.

• Take the time to do a sound warm-up such as The 11+ outlined in chapter 2 (page 18). Tangible rewards should be realized when a warm-up is included as a regular component of training. There are no guarantees when it is done infrequently. Most coaches are good at planning a training session, but neglect guiding the team through a good warm-up.

• The most dangerous part of soccer is tackling. Research has shown that the most dangerous tackles involve jumping, leading with one or both feet with the studs exposed, and coming from the front or the side. (Head-to-head contact is also dangerous. See the next item.) A simple axiom to remember is bad things happen when you leave your feet. Players should stay on their feet and not imitate what they see in professional games.

• Don't take head injury lightly. Head-to-head, elbow-to-head, ground-to-head, goalpost-to-head, or accidental ball-to-head impacts are dangerous. You cannot see a concussion like you can see a sprained ankle. A player who experiences one of these head contacts should be removed from the game immediately and not be allowed to resume play until everyone is sure about his safety. The best advice is: When in doubt, keep them out.

In the United States, many states are following the lead of Washington state, passing laws requiring written medical clearance before a player is allowed to return from a concussion. Don't mess around with head injuries. No game is that important.

• Exercise some common sense when it comes to training. For example, use age-appropriate balls. Older players shouldn't train with younger players. The younger ones will get run over or hit with high-velocity passes and shots. Next, the best predictor of an injury is a history of an injury, so an injured player should be fully recovered before returning. An incompletely healed minor injury often precedes a far more serious injury. Be smart and stand on a chair or ladder to put up or take down nets. The combination of jumping, gravity, rings, and net hooks is an invitation to a pretty severe laceration. Finally, never allow anyone to climb on goals. There have been serious injuries and even deaths because kids were playing on unanchored goalposts.

Knee Tuck Jump

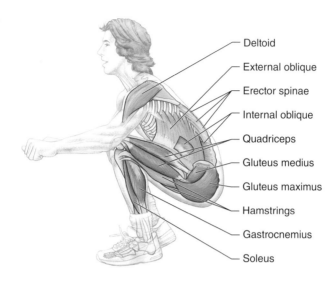

Deltoid
External oblique
Erector spinae
Internal oblique
Quadriceps
Gluteus medius
Gluteus maximus
Hamstrings
Gastrocnemius
Soleus

Execution

1. Choose shoes with good cushioning, and jump on a forgiving surface.
2. Using a two-foot takeoff, jump as high you can. Bring your knees as close to your trunk as possible. Use the arms for balance during flight.
3. Land softly to absorb the impact, and then quickly take off again. Spend as little time on the ground as possible. This exercise is simply reciprocal vertical jumps.

Muscles Involved

Primary: Quadriceps (vastus medialis, vastus lateralis, vastus intermedius, rectus femoris), gastrocnemius, soleus, gluteus maximus, gluteus medius, hip flexors (psoas major and minor, iliacus, rectus femoris, sartorius)

Secondary: Abdominal core (external oblique, internal oblique, transversus abdominis, rectus abdominis), erector spinae, hamstrings (biceps femoris, semitendinosus, semimembranosus), deltoid

Soccer Focus

Most books state that soccer is an endurance activity. With a 90-minute running clock (even though the ball is in play for only 70 minutes at most) and no stoppages, the game does have a significant endurance component. But games are won and lost by high-power bursts of activity—executing a short 10- to 20-yard (10 to 20 m) dash to the ball or outjumping an opponent for a corner, for example. Although these opportunities do not occur very frequently, players need to be ready when the time comes to execute high power output multiple times during a match. Many exercises train for high power output. Some involve an apparatus, and others are deceptively simple but very effective. Other exercises in this book involve jumping. Performing this exercise effectively requires you to jump as high as you can, pull your thighs up to your trunk, and then land softly and quietly. One jump is tough enough, but multiple jumps are very challenging. As you develop more power, you will find yourself jumping higher with each jump. As your legs develop local endurance, you will find yourself able to do more repetitions. Perform this exercise sparingly, when you have two or more days to recover before the coming match.

Repetitive Jump

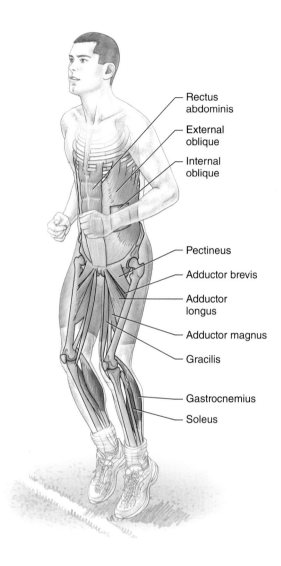

Rectus abdominis

External oblique

Internal oblique

Pectineus

Adductor brevis

Adductor longus

Adductor magnus

Gracilis

Gastrocnemius

Soleus

Execution

1. Stand facing or right beside the touchline or end line on the pitch.
2. Using a two-foot takeoff, jump back and forth or laterally just barely across the line.
3. Upon ground contact, jump back across the line as quickly as possible. This movement is very rapid, with little flight time and minimal ground-contact time.
4. Rather than count the number of ground contacts, do these jumps as rapidly as possible for a defined number of seconds, adding time as fitness improves.

Muscles Involved

Primary: Gastrocnemius, soleus

Secondary: Abdominal core, erector spinae, adductors (adductor longus, adductor magnus, adductor brevis, pectineus, gracilis)

Soccer Focus

Endurance, power, speed, agility—soccer requires virtually every aspect along the spectrum of fitness. Fast footwork is quickly becoming a part of skill training programs. You are asked to do a wide range of activities with as many ball contacts as possible in a short period of time. The player who has done these exercises knows that the physical demands of fast footwork training can be very tiring. Short, rapid touches in a very short time tax the ability of the body to produce energy rapidly. Exercises performed as fast as possible in a confined space prepare you for this kind of work.

VARIATIONS

This exercise simply takes you back and forth across a line on the ground. You can think up any number of variations such as traveling up and down the line; performing two touches on each side of the line; or imagining a shape on the ground and touching each corner, forward and back, adding a half spin. Use your imagination; just remember the keys—minimal flight and ground time. Increase the duration as fitness improves. You will be surprised at how fast you see improvements.

Depth Jump

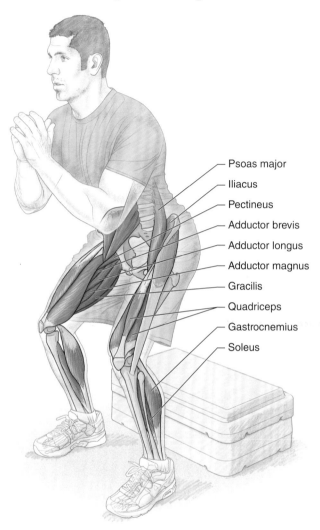

Psoas major
Iliacus
Pectineus
Adductor brevis
Adductor longus
Adductor magnus
Gracilis
Quadriceps
Gastrocnemius
Soleus

Execution

1. Choose a low box, about 12 inches (30 cm) tall.
2. Stand on the box with your legs about shoulder-width apart, hands and arms at your sides.
3. Step straight off the box. Land on both feet at the same time, bringing your hands up in front of you.
4. Absorb the impact of the landing by bending at the ankles, knees, and hips, sticking the landing so there are no adjustments to the impact.
5. Return to the box and repeat.

Muscles Involved

Primary: Hip flexors, quadriceps, gastrocnemius, soleus, adductors

Secondary: Erector spinae, abdominal core

Soccer Focus

Injury prevention is a theme of this book. Prevent injuries to keep playing and improve your game. At the core of injury prevention is neuromuscular control of the knees and the surrounding joints such as the ankles, hips, and trunk during demanding activities such as landing from a jump or cutting to change direction. Your goal for this exercise is to control the impact and not allow the knees to wobble right or left when landing. In addition, it is important to begin absorbing impact at the ankle and to not let the trunk waver during landing. If either of these surrounding joints shifts inappropriately, the knee must adjust, and this adjustment could put the knee in a poor position that could cause damage. Your coach should watch you when you perform this exercise to make sure your form is correct. Remember, these are single landings. Do not try to jump after stepping off the box.

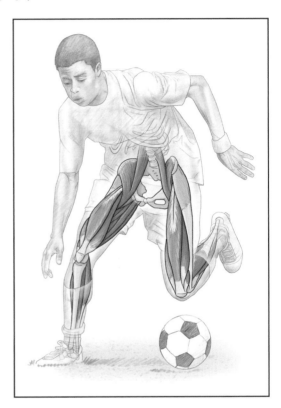

Speed Skater Lunge

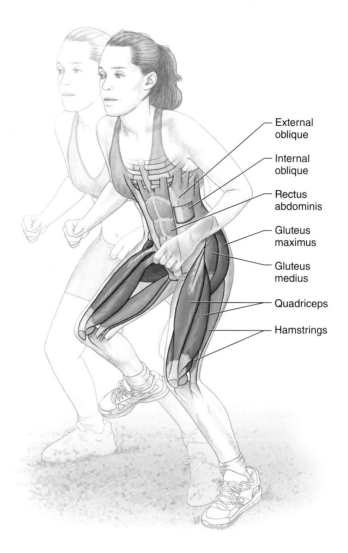

External oblique

Internal oblique

Rectus abdominis

Gluteus maximus

Gluteus medius

Quadriceps

Hamstrings

Execution

1. Stand with your legs about shoulder-width apart, with your hands on your hips or out to the sides for balance.
2. Keeping your trunk erect and straight, jump slightly and lunge to your right, landing on your right foot. Your left foot is off the ground, and you are balanced entirely on your right foot.
3. Pause briefly and repeat, jumping and lunging to your left.

Muscles Involved

Primary: Gluteus maximus, gluteus medius, quadriceps

Secondary: Erector spinae, hamstrings, abdominal core

Soccer Focus

This really is a whole-body exercise because it requires the legs to propel the sideways lunge; the core to stabilize the trunk during takeoff, flight, and landing; and the arms and shoulders for balance. With time you will begin to notice improvements in lateral quickness and agility. During a match, you don't do much conscious thinking about your movements. You may find yourself dribbling at speed when a defender you didn't notice pops up to challenge you. In an instant, you plant a foot and lunge far in the opposite direction while redirecting the ball into your path. But you never actually think about the movement; it just happens. The pace of your play and the ability to veer quickly and decisively away from your opponent can be drastically improved with simple exercises such as this. You will soon see an increase in the distance of the lateral lunge and the stability of landing as strength and neuromuscular control improve.

Floor Wiper

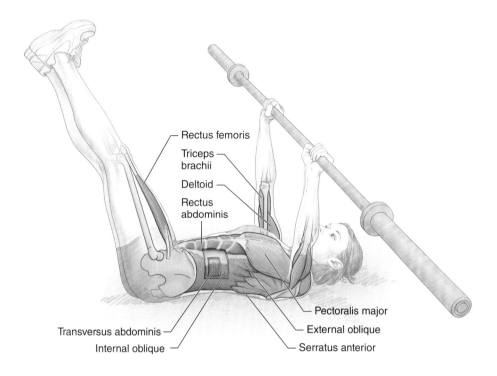

Rectus femoris

Triceps brachii

Deltoid

Rectus abdominis

Pectoralis major

External oblique

Serratus anterior

Transversus abdominis

Internal oblique

Execution

1. Lie on your back, holding an unweighted barbell above your chest. Arms are straight.
2. Without moving the barbell, raise your straight legs up toward one end of the barbell.
3. Keeping your legs straight, lower them back to the floor.
4. Repeat, raising your legs to the opposite end of the barbell. Moving the legs right and left counts as one repetition.

Muscles Involved

Primary: Abdominal core, rectus femoris, psoas major and minor, iliacus

Secondary: Sartorius, pectoralis major, triceps brachii, deltoid, serratus anterior

Soccer Focus

In the Soccer Focus section for the V-sit soccer ball pass (page 139), I mention a series of movies from the 1970s referred to as the Pepsi Pele movies. Within this excellent series of training films was a group of abdominal exercises that were part of a Brazilian circuit training protocol. This exercise is very similar, only instead of holding the ankles of a standing partner as the Brazilians did, you hold a barbell overhead and perform hip and trunk flexion combined with a little trunk rotation. Most of the abdominal exercises in the Pepsi Pele movies isolated the abs, but this exercise recruits multiple muscles of the core, making it a good bang for your exercise buck. Don't take this exercise lightly. It is quite challenging, especially when you realize the hard part of the action restricts your breathing. Don't forget that the bar stays overhead the entire time.

VARIATION

Floor Wiper With Dumbbells

This is the same exercise but with dumbbells. Holding a weight in each hand requires the arms and shoulders to balance each arm individually. Keep the arms overhead and the elbows extended as you perform the exercise as you would with a barbell.

Box Jump

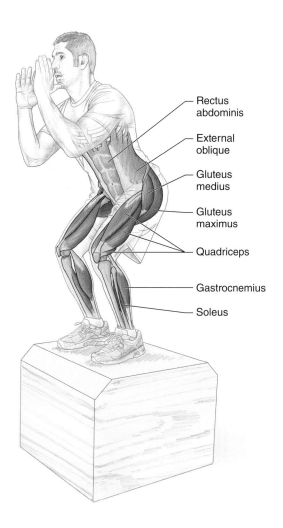

Rectus abdominis

External oblique

Gluteus medius

Gluteus maximus

Quadriceps

Gastrocnemius

Soleus

Execution

1. Stand in front of a sturdy box—one that will not tip over—that is midshin to knee height.

2. Using a two-foot takeoff, jump high onto the box, landing on both feet. Don't jump just high enough to land on the box. Jump higher so you are coming down on the box.

3. Jump back to your starting point, landing softly and quietly to absorb the force of the landing.

4. Repeat in a continuous, nonstop motion. Start with 5 to 10 seconds, and add time as fitness improves.

Muscles Involved

Primary: Quadriceps, gluteus maximus, gluteus medius, gastrocnemius, soleus

Secondary: Abdominal core, erector spinae, hip flexors

Soccer Focus

Modern soccer is a mix of high-power-output activities surrounded by more endurance-oriented running. A sought-after trait is the desire and ability of each player to press everywhere on the field. Upon losing possession, the player, often with one or two teammates, will press the opponent on any number of levels (e.g., to immediately regain possession, to close down in order to occupy the opponent and keep the ball in front, to rapidly close down to force an errant pass, or to close down a player and delay forward movement, allowing teammates to recover). In each case, pressing the opponent requires a fast, controlled approach featuring a short-term period of very high power output. This kind of work is very intense, but it can have important and nearly immediate outcomes when the opponent makes a mistake and a teammate collects the ball. The challenge is to develop sufficient fitness in order to press, and press appropriately, when the need arises. Nearly every coach will say how hard it is to get a player to press when that player has lost possession of the ball. Part of this is frustration or disappointment at having lost possession, but it also may stem from a lack of fitness. Jumping exercises such as this require a very high power output that when used in combination with similar work on and off the ball should help put a team into the position of being very effective at pressing.

Romanian Deadlift

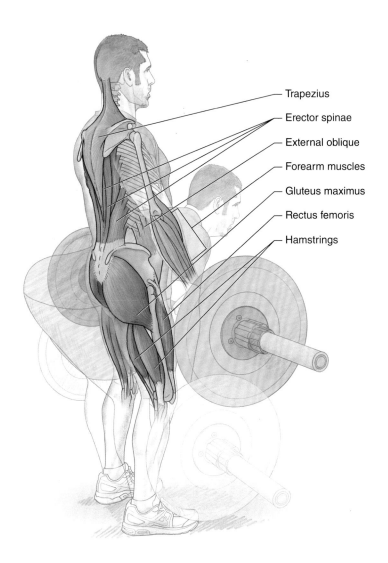

Trapezius

Erector spinae

External oblique

Forearm muscles

Gluteus maximus

Rectus femoris

Hamstrings

Execution

1. With the barbell on the floor, stand with your feet flat on the floor, shoulder-width apart or slightly less, and toes under the bar and pointed slightly out.

2. Move into a deep squat. With the arms straight, grasp the bar in an overhand grip, palms down. Your back should be flat or slightly arched. Pull your shoulders back and your chest forward.

3. Look forward and take a breath. Pushing through your heels and contracting your quadriceps and gluteals, pull the weight off the floor. Keep your back flat and the bar close. Stand erect, but don't lock your knees. Exhale.

4. Inhale and slowly lower the bar by returning to the starting position.

Muscles Involved

Primary: Erector spinae, rectus femoris, gluteus maximus, hamstrings

Secondary: Scapular stabilizers (such as trapezius), rectus abdominis, external oblique, internal oblique, forearm muscles (mostly wrist and finger flexors including flexor carpi radialis and ulnaris, palmaris longus, flexor digitorum superficialis and profundus, and flexor pollicis longus), vastus lateralis, vastus medialis, vastus intermedius

Soccer Focus

The deadlift is a whole-body exercise found in nearly every training manual across the sporting spectrum. It demands power output from the legs, hips, trunk, and back. If you have never done this lift before, you may think it looks easy, but the use of a barbell increases its complexity by making a smooth motion more difficult. It is a good idea to get some personal instruction to ensure you are doing this lift correctly and safely. Rounding the back during the lift exposes the intervertebral discs to possible herniation, so keep your head up. Looking at the bar leads to a rounded back. Also, do not try to flex the forearms during this lift because it can place unnecessary strain on the biceps. Posture is the key. Don't take any shortcuts with the deadlift.

ADDITIONAL RESOURCES

From FIFA

Health and Fitness for the Female Football Player: www.fifa.com/mm/
document/afdeveloping/medical/ffb_gesamt_e_20035.pdf
F-MARC Nutrition for Football: www.fifa.com/mm/document/
afdeveloping/medical/nutrition_booklet_e_1830.pdf
The 11+: http://f-marc.com/11plus/index.html

From the National Strength and Conditioning Association (NSCA)

Position statement on youth resistance training: www.nsca-lift.org/
Publications/YouthResistanceTrainingUpdatedPosition2.pdf
Position statements on other aspects of resistance training:
www.nsca-lift.org/Publications/posstatements.shtml

From Human Kinetics

Resistance training catalogs: www.humankinetics.com/
personalstrengthtraining
www.humankinetics.com/youngathletes

EXERCISE FINDER

Legs: Complete Power

Whole-Body Training for Soccer

ABOUT THE AUTHOR

Donald T. Kirkendall is uniquely positioned to author *Soccer Anatomy*. He earned a PhD in exercise physiology from The Ohio State University and went on to teach human anatomy, physiology, and exercise physiology as a faculty member at the University of Wisconsin at Lacrosse and Illinois State University. In 1995 he was recruited to join the sports medicine program at Duke University Medical Center and then at the University of North Carolina at Chapel Hill. His research interests focus on sports medicine and physical performance with an emphasis on team sports—especially soccer. Since 1997 he has written a sport science column for the monthly magazine *Southern Soccer Scene*.

Dr. Kirkendall began competing in soccer during middle school and continued to play during high school and junior college and at Ohio University, where he competed in the NCAA tournament. He continues to play today in adult recreational leagues. He has coached soccer at various levels from U10 youth leagues to assistant coach at Ball State University in Indiana and earned the USSF B coaching license.

Dr. Kirkendall is a member of FIFA's Medical Assessment and Research Centre (F-MARC) based in Zurich, Switzerland. The Fédération Internationale de Football Association (FIFA) is the international governing body for soccer. F-MARC conducts and collaborates on medical studies to reduce soccer injuries and promote soccer as a healthful activity. Dr. Kirkendall is also a member of U.S. Soccer's Medical Advisory Committee. Because of these affiliations and his expertise in applying sport science concepts to soccer, he is in demand around the world as a speaker on soccer-related sport science topics. He frequently lectures at coaching clinics and to local and national coaching organizations, and he has lectured to audiences in all six of FIFA's confederations.

ANATOMY SERIES

Each book in the *Anatomy Series* provides detailed, full-color anatomical illustrations of the muscles in action and step-by-step instructions that detail perfect technique and form for each pose, exercise, movement, stretch, and stroke.

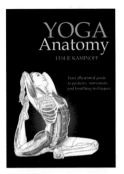

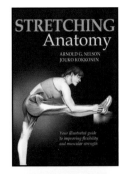

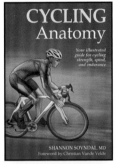

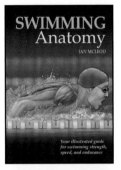

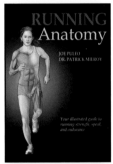

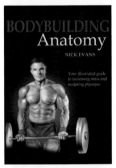

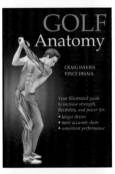

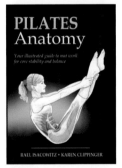

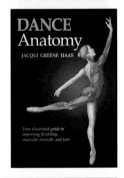

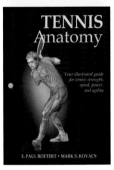

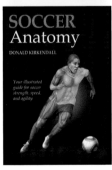

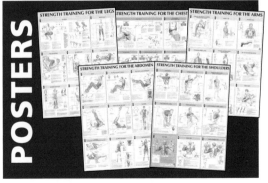

To place your order, U.S. customers call TOLL FREE **1-800-747-4457**
In Canada call 1-800-465-7301 • In Europe call +44 (0) 113 255 5665 • In Australia call 08 8372 0999
In New Zealand call 0800 222 062 • or visit **www.HumanKinetics.com/Anatomy**

HUMAN KINETICS
The Premier Publisher for Sports & Fitness
P.O. Box 5076, Champaign, IL 61825-5076